T0300237

Routledge Revivals

Trade with Communist Countries

First published in 1960 *Trade with Communist Countries* presents an important research report for the first time covering the essential facts and drawing conclusions on East/West trading possibilities. Two authors combine to ensure an authoritative coverage of the many facets of this complex problem. Alec Nove examines the organisation of Soviet trade against the background of domestic economic planning and assesses the prospects for greater East/West trade. In course of his review he discusses such important questions as rates of exchange, bilateralism, and strategic controls. Desmond Donnelly surveys the prospects and practical methods of trading with Communist countries and examines the political consequences of freer trading relations between capitalist and Communist countries. Rich in archival resources this book is a must read for scholars and researchers of economics, economic history, Soviet history, and international trade.

Trade with Communist Countries

Alec Nove and Desmond Donnelly

Routledge
Taylor & Francis Group

First published in 1960
by Hutchinson & Co (Publishers) Ltd.

This edition first published in 2021 by Routledge
2 Park Square, Milton Park, Abingdon, Oxon, OX14 4RN
and by Routledge
605 Third Avenue, New York, NY 10017

Routledge is an imprint of the Taylor & Francis Group, an informa business

Publisher's Note
The publisher has gone to great lengths to ensure the quality of this reprint but points
out that some imperfections in the original copies may be apparent.

Disclaimer
The publisher has made every effort to trace copyright holders and welcomes
correspondence from those they have been unable to contact.

A Library of Congress record exists under LCCN: 60004477

ISBN: 978-1-032-15261-5 (hbk)
ISBN: 978-1-003-24332-8 (ebk)
ISBN: 978-1-032-15262-2 (pbk)

Book DOI 10.4324/9781003243328

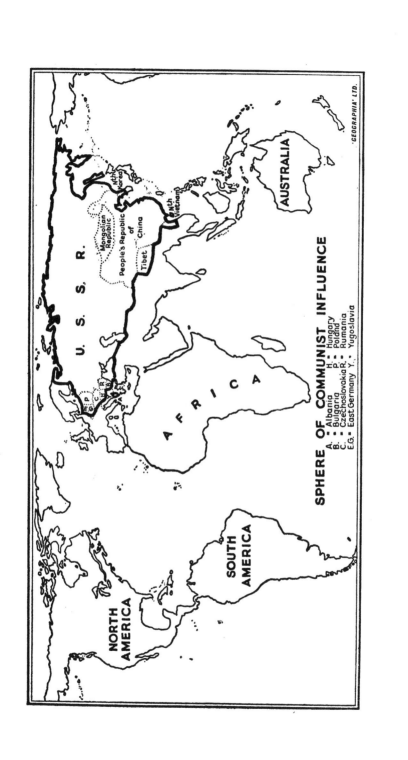

SPHERE OF COMMUNIST INFLUENCE

A. = Albania   H. = Hungary
B. = Bulgaria   P. = Poland
C. = Czechoslovakia R. = Rumania
E.G. = East Germany Y. = Yugoslavia

U. S. S. R.

Mongolian
Republic

People's Republic
of
China

North
Korea

Tibet

North
Vietnam

AUSTRALIA

AFRICA

NORTH
AMERICA

SOUTH
AMERICA

'GEOGRAPHIA' LTD.

Trade with Communist Countries

ALEC NOVE
Reader in Russian Social and Economic
Studies in the University of London

DESMOND DONNELLY
Member of Parliament

Published for
THE INSTITUTE OF ECONOMIC AFFAIRS
by
HUTCHINSON OF LONDON

HUTCHINSON & CO (*Publishers*) LTD

178-202 Great Portland Street, London, W1

London Melbourne Sydney
Auckland Bombay Toronto
Johannesburg New York

First published 1960

Printed in Great Britain by
Merritt & Hatcher Ltd., High Wycombe and London

Contents

Sphere of Communist influence   *Frontispiece*

Foreword by J. B. Scott, D.F.C.   9

BOOK I by Alec Nove—The Economics of East-West Trade

Part I   Principles and Prospects

Chapter I   THE FRAMEWORK OF INTERNAL TRADE
  1. The scope of the work   13
  2. A state monopoly   13
  3. The planning process   14
  4. The price system   17
  5. The priority of growth, and inefficiency   19
  6. How foreign trade fits into the plan   21
  7. Divorce between internal and external prices   23
  8. How a trade corporation works   24

Chapter II   THE RELATIONS BETWEEN EXTERNAL TRADE
              AND INTERNAL PLANNING
  1. Criticism of the Soviet planning and price system   29
  2. The value of external prices for internal planning   31
  3. The conflict between political control and freedom to trade 31
  4. The use of markets in Yugoslavia   32

Chapter III   DISCRIMINATION IN EXTERNAL TRADE
  1. A consequence of the planning process   33
  2. The attitude of the West   35
  3. The Soviet attitude   35

Chapter IV   THE LIMITATIONS ON EXTERNAL TRADE
  1. Shortage of means of payment   39
  2. The urge to autarky   40
  3. Unhelpfulness from the West?   40
  4. The 'strategic controls'   43
  5. The role of credits   44
  6. Moscow gold   44
  7. The prospect for rouble convertibility   45

Chapter V THE PROSPECT FOR INCREASED EXTERNAL TRADE

    1. Shortage of capital goods for under-developed countries   47
    2. The need for imports   48
    3. Exports from the East   50
    4. China   51

Chapter VI A POLITICO-ECONOMIC APPRAISAL

    1. The American view   55
    2. The counter-arguments   56
    3. A reason for hope   57

PART II   The Economic Structure of Communist Countries

A   The Economic Administrative Regions ('Sovnarkhozy')
     of the Union of Soviet Socialist Republics   61

B   Organisational Structure of an Economic Council
     (Sverdlovsk Sovnarkhoz)   87

PART III   External Trade Statistics

A	Soviet External Trade	Table I	By Country	90
		Table II	By Commodity	92
B	East German External Trade	Table I	By Groups of Countries	94
		Table II	By Country	94
		Table III	By Commodity	96
C	Polish External Trade	Table I	By Country	98
		Table II	By Commodity	99
D	Czechoslovakian External Trade	Table I	By Groups of Countries	101
		Table II	By Country	102
		Table III	By Commodity	103

BOOK II by Desmond Donnelly—The Mechanics of East-West Trade

Part I   The Background

Chapter I PROBLEMS OF TRADING WITH COMMUNISTS

    1. Introduction   107
    2. Foreign trade within the Soviet bloc   108
    3. The strategic embargo   112
    4. Contract terms   113
    5. Advertising   114
    6. Conclusion   115

Chapter II   THE SOVIET UNION

    1. Background   117
    2. System of trade   121
    3. Promotion of trade and value of personal contacts   122
    4. Travel facilities   122
    5. Seven Year Plan   123
    6. Anglo-Soviet Trade Treaty   124
        Five Year Trade Agreement   125
        'Possible Imports' from UK to the USSR, 1960-64   128

Chapter III   THE EAST EUROPEAN COUNTRIES

    1. General   131
    2. Poland   133
    3. Czechoslovakia   136
    4. Hungary   139
    5. Eastern Germany   142
    6. Bulgaria, Roumania, Albania   144
    7. Conclusion.   144
        Map—Donnelly's Travels   146

Chapter IV   CHINA

    1. General   147
    2. The system   150
    3. Travel arrangements   151
    6. Chinese economic planning   152

Chapter V   JUGOSLAVIA

    1. The system   154
    2. General   157

Chapter VI   THE PROSPECTS FOR EAST-WEST TRADE   159

Part II   Trading Corporations and the commodities they handle

A   The Soviet Union   165
B   Poland   167
C   Czechoslovakia   169
D   Roumania   171
E   Bulgaria   172
F   China   173

Index   181

The Institute of Economic Affairs

The Institute was formed in 1956 as an educational trust. Its chief aim is to raise the standard of economic discussion by spreading understanding of basic principles, expressing them in plain language, relating them to everyday problems, and distinguishing between the economic requirements of a free society and the political expedients that often govern public policy.

Its work is assisted by an advisory council which includes Sir Oscar Hobson, Colin Clark, Professor Stanley Dennison, Graham Hutton, Professor John Jewkes, Professor Eric Nash, George Schwartz and Lord Granchester. The Institute is directed by Ralph Harris, and its publications are supervised by Arthur Seldon.

For *Trade with Communist Countries*, the Institute invited two authors: Mr. Alec Nove, a leading authority on the Russian economy and Mr. Desmond Donnelly, who writes with personal knowledge of the possibilities and problems of trade with Russia, China and other Communist countries. They write from different points of view, but combine to produce a volume that will be valued not only by business men and students of economics but also by a wider audience concerned about the West's relations with the East. The Institute is not committed to the analysis or conclusions, but it commends them for public discussion and consideration.

The Institute is independent of any political party or group. It is financed by voluntary contributions from individuals, companies and organisations, and from sales of its publications. Subscription is open to all interested individuals and organisations: associate membership (individual or corporate) is at the invitation of the Trustees.

Further information is contained in a brochure available from: The General Director, Institute of Economic Affairs, Seven Hobart Place, London, S.W.1. (Sloane 9251).

Foreword

by J. B. Scott, D.F.C.

Overseas Sales Director, Crompton Parkinson Ltd

It has been my privilege, during the last six years, to participate in much of the work that has been done in reconstituting commercial relations between the United Kingdom and the USSR, and because this is so it gives me very great pleasure to contribute a foreword to this book. The two authors who have joined together in this venture, both friends of mine, are well fitted to their task, Mr. Nove by his intimate knowledge of the Russian scene and the Russian people, and Mr. Donnelly by the wide acquaintance with political affairs which he has gained as a Member of Parliament and by the knowledge of the world he has acquired in the course of extensive travels.

I and others who have been engaged in trade with Communist countries have gained our knowledge the hard way, by experience: the experience sometimes of disappointment and frustration but often of encouragement and success. If such a book as this had existed ten years ago we should have been saved from some of the disappointments and helped immensely towards the successes. For, writing each from his own special knowledge, the two authors have compressed a great deal of information into a modest compass, and it is the information needed by the business man who contemplates trading with the Communist world.

But if this book had been written six years ago it would, of course, have been a different book. Russia, China and the East European countries have all experienced changes during that period, their institutions have been shaped and re-shaped, and, especially in Russia, the material standard of living has improved markedly, with manifold consequences upon the texture of society and the emphasis placed on different economic needs. But we in the West have also changed and are still changing. Revolutions need be neither sudden nor violent, and we are ourselves experiencing a silent revolution in our way of life and thought. Neither in the East nor the West is the pattern set for all time, nor can it ever be. The tragedy of the recent past is that in the course of world-wide change there has come to be a wide divergence between the fundamental thinking of those who direct the operations of production and exchange in Communist countries and their counterparts in the West, as a result of which there has been a great deal of misunderstanding and suspicion. No-one can foresee with certainty what will be the shape of business in the East or the West a few generations hence; but today there are gulfs of misunderstanding and, in order to bridge them, techniques of negotiation and presentation must be learned.

Yet at two levels the essential factors remain unaltered. At the basic economic level the advantages of international trade remain what they were, and the natural needs and resources of the various regions in East and West exist as facts irrespective of systems or ideology. And at the personal level business is transacted by human beings whose essential nature, strengths and weaknesses are what they have always been. It is in the methods and the machinery that lie between the personal contact and the basic need that institutions and systems have diverged so widely between East and West.

For two very good reasons we in the United Kingdom should go forward in the search for understanding and confidence. Firstly, we live by trade, and without trade life would be impossible for us. There are few regions of the world where the potential for trade with the United Kingdom so vastly exceeds the actual and current level as is the case with the Communist countries. The second compelling reason is that no country in the world has more vital interest than we have in the building of a stable world peace. Such a peace involves understanding and mutual respect. Trade, bringing at one and the same time a state of interdependence and a wealth of personal contacts, is the surest means of fostering this understanding, and the industrialist and the merchant are today ambassadors of peace.

But whether or not the individual trader or manufacturer is aware of the deeper significance of his actions, whether he is merely looking for profitable business or is impelled by an idealistic will to work for peace and understanding, makes no difference to his first questions. How is he to start? With whom is he to make contact? What basic information does he need? Ought he to travel to the territory to which he wants to sell? If he does, what should he do on arrival? These, and many others, are the questions which the authors of this book have so ably answered

Book I
The Economics of East-West Trade

Part I
Principles and Prospects

THE AUTHOR

Alec Nove was born in Leningrad 44 years ago and left Russia as a child. He graduated at the London School of Economics, served in the army 1939-46 (ending as a Major) and was a Civil Servant from 1947 to 1957. He is now Reader in Russian Social and Economic Studies, University of London, and has made three visits to Russia 1955, 1956, 1959.

CHAPTER I

The Framework of Internal Trade

1. *The scope of the work*

How does Soviet foreign trade 'fit' into Soviet planning and economic life generally? Who decides what should be imported or exported, and on what basis do they so decide? What, if anything, have relative costs and prices to do with the decision to trade? Who decides what the prices of Soviet exports are to be, or the prices at which imports are sold in the home market? What meaning, if any, have such concepts as 'most-favoured-nation treatment' in trade with the USSR and its allies? Is dumping a typical feature of Soviet trade practices? These are the sort of questions that will be discussed below. To some of them it will prove possible to give more or less precise answers. Others will be discussed in more general terms, because no definite answer is possible, either because we do not know what happens, or because the situation is in process of change. It is, indeed, important to note that the principles by which Soviet bloc countries conduct their foreign trade have been discussed and reconsidered in a number of these countries, so that one should not take the existing situation as necessarily fixed for all time.

2. *A state monopoly*

An essential feature of foreign trade organisation in all the Soviet countries is that it is a state monopoly. All commercial transactions with foreign countries are carried out by trading corporations set up by the State and administratively supervised by the Ministry of Foreign Trade. On page 165 will be found a list of these corporations, and a description of their functions, as known at the beginning of 1959. They are, of course, subject to change. Other Soviet bloc countries have corporations bearing different names and with different product coverage, but the general principles are the same, although the direct role of state enterprises in foreign trade transactions is greater in some countries than in others. In the USSR the state monopoly of foreign trade was decreed as long ago as 1918, and the trade corporations acquired their present shape in the early thirties. Most of the actual commercial work abroad is carried out by permanent trade delegations (*torgpredstva*) with diplomatic status, located in foreign countries. These delegations would naturally include nominees of trade corporations most directly concerned in trade with that particular country. Thus the delegation in London has a timber expert with direct links with the *Exportles* corporation, which organises the sales of Soviet timber.

3. *The planning process*

Before discussing in any great detail the way in which trade is actually conducted, it is desirable to turn to the more general background. It is common knowledge that trade in a Soviet country is an integral part of a planned economy. Therefore the trade corporations themselves work within and to a plan. Therefore an outline of the planning process is an essential prerequisite to understanding what they do and why they do it.

The general economic long-term plan is elaborated by the State Planning Commission (Gosplan), on policy lines determined nominally by the Soviet Government and in practice by the leadership of the Communist Party. Long-term objectives are published in the form of five-year plans, or as in the present case, of seven-year plans. Naturally, these take into account any unexpected successes or failures, and the long-term plans are always amended upwards or downwards in the course of execution. Thus, for instance, the seven-year plan (1959-65) is being speeded up, as a number of key regions have announced their intention of fulfilling it by 1964 or even earlier.

While the planning is essentially a central responsibility, it is obvious that a great deal has to be initiated at lower rungs of the administrative ladder. Each productive enterprise or firm begins the process of planning by submitting its own draft plan. Since the economic reforms of 1957, practically all industrial enterprises of any importance are controlled by Regional Economic Councils; the USSR is divided into 104 economic regions, each headed by such a council. Each of the councils drafts a plan for its region, and sends the draft up the hierarchical ladder. The next rung depends on whether the given region is co-extensive with a federal republic (e.g. a small republic, such as Georgia or Belorussia); if it is, then the republic's plan is submitted to the all-Union Gosplan in Moscow. If, on the other hand, the given republic has many economic regions (Russia proper has 68, the Ukraine 11), the regional draft goes first to the Gosplan of the appropriate federal republic. The latter co-ordinates, amends, and finally submits a republican draft to the all-union Gosplan in Moscow. The latter makes its own amendments. There is much argument and many journeys to Moscow from the provincial centres to plead for changes, or for the cancellation of amendments made by the centre to local projects. Needless to say, the regional and republican plans are made in the knowledge of the general economic policy of the centre, but there are many local axes to grind. One of the more common features of Soviet planning has been the tendency for the number of claims for investment funds greatly to exceed the amounts available for investment. This is very largely due to the fact that capital investments in the USSR are financed by outright grants, mostly from the state budget, and appear to cost the recipients nothing. Small wonder that they ask for as much as possible, or that Gosplan makes cuts.

Other 'Soviet' countries face somewhat different problems of regional control, since they (with the exception of China) are much smaller, and consequently can be more easily managed from the centre. All have a Gosplan, or some equivalent body, charged with co-ordinating the national plan. However, the various branches of industry are generally controlled by central departments (ministries), who administer the branch under their control and are headed by a minister who is a member of the government. This was, indeed the system which operated in the USSR itself until the reforms of 1957*. In Czechoslovakia important functions reside with the

---

* Before 1957, most industrial enterprises in the USSR were subject not to the regional councils but to *ministries*, and these were directly (or, in the case of federal-republic ministries indirectly) under the central government. The plans and claims of the various ministries were co-ordinated by Gosplan. For a number

so-called 'trusts', which group together on a quasi-federal basis all enterprises within one industrial sector. There is now a good deal of freedom to experiment in the various countries of the Soviet bloc.

The individual enterprise, which actually does the productive work, is a *state* institution, in that its assets are owned by the state. Its manager is appointed (since 1957) by the regional economic council and his duty is to fulfil—or, better still, overfulfil—the output plan laid down for his enterprise. If he does this, he will be rewarded. It is also his duty to make a profit, or more precisely to make a larger profit (or a smaller loss) than was planned, since the profit he will make is largely a function of the price at which he can sell, and this is fixed by the state (more about prices in a moment). However, the primary task is plan fulfilment.** This is logical, since, where prices are fixed by the state, they cannot act as market indicators, and consequently, it would not be sensible in such an institutional setting to rely on the profit motive to persuade the managers to do the right things.

The manager has to purchase the goods and services, which he needs to fulfil his plan, from other state enterprises, at prices which are also fixed by the state. In most instances, the materials and components he buys are subject to allocation by the planning agencies. For example, in order to buy steel or timber, the manager requires an allocation certificate, which is issued only if he shows that he must have steel or timber to fulfil the plan. A complex set of technical coefficients determines how much of these or other 'allocated' commodities he is entitled to. It is these allocation decisions, rather than relative prices, which ultimately determine who gets what materials; however, allocations always depend indirectly on applications, even if these are cut or amended, and so the initiative of the enterprise manager does have an effect on what actually happens, though his formal rights of decision are restricted. This is a point of some importance which is often overlooked by analysts of the Soviet economy, and applies, as we shall see, also

---

of reasons which it is unnecessary to discuss here, nearly all these separate ministries have been abolished, and regional economic councils created. There also existed, and exist, productive enterprises, usually small, run by local Soviets, as well as producers' co-operative workshops. They play a negligible role in anything to do with foreign trade and will be ignored here.

** However, in the USSR, bonuses for output plan fulfilment were, late in 1959, related to achieving or exceeding the cost reduction plan.

to foreign trade. One should not deduce from the formal centralisation of various decisions that the men on the spot are mere yes-men and that everything really is decided in some office in Moscow without reference to anyone.

Agricultural production has some peculiar features—such as collective farms—which need not detain us in the present context. Apart from some sales direct to consumers in free markets in the cities, all produce not consumed on the farm is disposed of to state wholesale agencies, at prices fixed by the state. The state can decide the quantities of given types of produce it wishes to procure from the farms, and appropriate orders can be issued through republican and regional authorities.

The basis of the entire planning system is essentially quantitative. Many of the decisions arise from a somewhat elementary form of what economists call 'input-output analysis'; they are technical consequentials of other decisions. Considerations of money have entered the process of decision-making largely in the context of choice between alternative means of fulfilling *given* requirements (e.g. is it cheaper to use natural gas or coal for thermal power stations in Moscow? Is it more rational to build thermal or hydro-electric power stations?), or as a rough check on the efficiency of productive enterprises. However, even this limited use of cost analysis was made very difficult by the arbitrary nature of prices.

4. *The price system*

Prices in the Soviet Union are of several types and are based on somewhat different principles. Leaving out of account the very complicated issue of agricultural prices, which has been bedevilled by political and social considerations, let us examine the price system.

In the first place, there is the 'enterprise' wholesale price, at which an industrial enterprise sells its products. This is, in almost all important instances, fixed by the government and is intended to cover the average cost of production, with a profit margin of a few per cent. Note that this is the average cost, not the marginal cost, so that some producers inevitably make losses and are expected to do so. The term 'cost' covers wages, social insurance contributions, purchases of goods and services from other enterprises, and depreciation. Apart from quite minor items, such as interest on

B

short-term credits, this exhausts the list. Basic capital, being state-owned, is not charged for. In practice, thanks to very large differences between costs in different enterprises and to errors in price fixing, the factory wholesale price sometimes permits very high profits, or causes production at a heavy loss. An example from the steel industry will illustrate the point:

Factory	Wholesale price (*Roubles per ton*)	Costs of production (*Roubles per ton*)	Profit or loss (% *of costs*)
Kuznetsk	330	220	+50
Azov	330	329	+ 0·3
Transcaucasian	330	488	−32·4
Cherepovets	330	613	−46·2

Source A. G. Zverev: *Voprosy Natsionalnovo Dokhoda i Finansov SSSR* (Moscow, 1958) p. 196.

In the case of most 'producers' goods' supplied by one enterprise to another, this enterprise wholesale price, plus wholesalers' margin where applicable, is the price at which these goods are transferred to other user enterprises. However, tax is charged on oil, electricity and on certain raw materials for the light and food industries.

The other major category is, of course, retail prices. These are influenced by two interconnected factors. Firstly, retail prices, in the absence of rationing, must tend to be fixed so that supply and demand are approximately in balance, so that queues are not too long, and the consumers' goods get sold. (It is true that queues do exist, but at least the principle is that they should not.) Producers' goods are generally subject to allocation, i.e. rationed, and so need not be priced to equate demand with supply. Consumers, however, are free to choose, and this must influence price formation even though the prices themselves are fixed by the authorities. Secondly, consumers must pay, through a higher mark-up on consumer goods, the major part of the state's expenditure on investment, defence, social services and so on, since direct taxation is quite small and may soon become even smaller. This mark-up usually takes the form of turnover tax, and the bulk of this tax is paid on consumers' goods or on materials entering into their production, with oil and electricity the only exceptions of any consequence.* This is one reason for the great difficulty which faces us in trying to find a 'real value' for the Soviet rouble. By and large in comparison with any western

* In some countries (Poland, for instance) a low rate of turnover tax (1 per cent) is applied over a wide range of producers' goods for 'control' purposes.

country, consumers' goods are relatively dear and producers' goods (steel, engineering, etc.) relatively cheap. The citizen pays through retail prices for much of the investment expenditure in heavy industry, and in some years (in some instances even today) prices in heavy industry did not even cover the bare costs of production and had to be subsidised. The higher prices of many consumers' goods reflect, in addition to turnover tax, the greater relative inefficiency in the consumers' goods industries: the Soviet planners have deliberately concentrated the best machinery and the best managers in heavy industry, and so the Soviet textile or furniture industry is poorly equipped and poorly run in comparison.

5. *The priority of growth, and inefficiency*

Soviet economists have been pointing out that the planning and price system involves a good deal of inefficiency. Prices often bear little logical relationship to costs, and indeed costs are themselves irrational, because neither capital charges nor rents appear in them. Thus, changes in the pattern of demand either find no reflection whatever in prices, or do so only if a government office takes a decision to that effect, which it seldom does. As a result, the price system is of little use as a 'transmitter' to the producers of the requirements of the users, and this incessantly involves the planners and administrators in a multitude of detailed decisions about exactly what each factory should produce.

None the less, each enterprise has some range of choice in the assortment of its product and, since the main task is to fulfil the plan, the product mix is adjusted to the measurement of plan fulfilment, instead of to the requirements of consumers. Thus, if the plan is in tons, goods are unnecessarily heavy. To correct such deviations, the planners must repeatedly intervene.

For example, Khrushchev criticised industry for making excessively heavy chandeliers, giving the reason: that the 'chandeliers plan' was expressed in tons. Another example may be cited from a decree on consumer durables (*Pravda*, 16 October 1959), which lays down a number of detailed specifications in an effort to order industry to meet the requirements of consumers; thus industry's apparently incurable habit of producing ugly dark red lamp-shades with long tassels is now to be broken by a decree; after a certain date their manufacture is to be prohibited. Thus the conversion of consumer preference into production decisions, even in so detailed a matter, required an order signed jointly by the council of ministers and the central committee of the Communist Party, which seems a clumsy procedure. Similar troubles have been met with in other 'Soviet' countries, and a very interesting book describing Hungarian experience in these matters has recently appeared in an English translation.*

Production decisions have to be linked with the appropriate allocations of materials and of investment funds, and this creates acute complications in the various planning offices which have to co-ordinate a vast number of decisions which affect each other but are necessarily located in different branches of the planning machine. The natural tendency in these circumstances is towards self-sufficiency, departmental or local. Thus, when economic ministries ran industry, each ministry (e.g. the ministry of coal, of power, metallurgy, of heavy machine building) would endeavour to rely as much as possible on its 'own' sources of supply; it would put up workshops to manufacture its own components, it would quarry its own materials for its own construction organisation, and so on. The abolition of these ministries in 1957 broke up these self-sufficient empires, but the tendency now is towards *regional* autarky for exactly the same reasons; within the region one can at least be sure that the necessary resources for carrying out the plan can be made available. This tendency is strongly denounced by the authorities, since it leads to neglect of orders from other regions.** However, it is unintentionally encouraged by judging the regional economic councils primarily for fulfilling and overfulfilling their own gross output plans.

Indeed, much that is wrong with economic organisation in the USSR is a direct consequence of giving top priority to, and top rewards for, quantitative overfulfilment of plans, i.e. to rapid growth as such rather than to any very careful counting of costs. Of course, if growth at any cost is the primary object of economic activity, these procedures have their logic. But that is another story.

*Janos Kornai: *Overcentralization in Economic Administration,* Oxford University Press, 1959.

**For instance, in *Pravda* 20 May, 1958, and many other newspapers and periodicals. The Regional Councils are threatened with punishment for failing to fulfil contracts for 'outside' deliveries. However, this provision cannot compel them to sign the contracts in the first place, unless under detailed central orders.

The essential points to note are that planning is primarily quantitative, that prices and profitability play a subordinate role in decision-making, that increases in gross output receive the highest rewards, and finally that the system of material allocation is always subject to great strains which lead to a tendency towards autarky within the functional or regional 'empires' into which, for reasons of administrative necessity, the economy must be divided. It is important to realise that this tendency towards autarky exists *within* the Soviet Union as well as in dealings between the USSR and other countries, and that it is to some extent inherent in the process of planning itself, though (as will be shown) this by no means excludes expansion of trade from present levels by substantial percentages.

6. *How foreign trade fits into the plan*

Having given some account of the internal planning and pricing mechanism, we must now see how foreign trade fits into it, dealing first with the Soviet Union, then modifying our pictures somewhat to take other Soviet bloc countries into account.

The plan must include the importation of a number of commodities, the need for which cannot be met from within the USSR. Some, like cocoa, natural rubber or jute, cannot be grown there for climatic reasons. Others, such as wool, copper, ships or chemical machinery, are produced in insufficient quantities to cover known plan requirements. No doubt Gosplan, in conjunction with the Ministry of Foreign Trade, draws up a list of essential imports. Then there are other imports of a less essential kind, which are none-the-less useful and which it would pay the Soviet Union to purchase under bilateral agreements: these would include a number of foodstuffs, manufactured consumers' goods and so on. The central authorities doubtless receive more applications for imported goods than can be paid for, and the actual plan must be based on estimated export earnings. These, in turn, depend on the goods that can be made available for export, the prices at which they can be sold, and the nature of the currencies earned. In many cases there are competing demands for exportable goods at home. For example, timber which could be exported to Great Britain is urgently needed for building projects in Russia. Gosplan (and, in the last resort, the Communist Party leaders) must decide in such cases who is to go short, whether the export earnings are the more urgent in this particular instance. Out of all this there finally emerges an import and export plan, linked with the internal plans for the given period.

These procedures appear to be wholly centralised, and in a formal sense it is always so, since no Soviet local authority or enterprise is entitled to engage in foreign trade. However, here as elsewhere, the central decisions are often a consequence of applications from below. For instance, imports of machinery are affected by the requirements of enterprises, or of regional economic councils, who consult 'their' enterprises. This is why advertising in journals circulating in the USSR is by no means useless. Thus the periodical *British Industry and British Engineering* (published in Russian in London) receives inquiries from chief engineers and other local technical officials. It is true that the enterprises in question cannot place orders in England. They can, however, submit a statement of their needs to higher authority and thereby influence the foreign trade plan and, in the last resort, the behaviour of the foreign trade corporation responsible for importing the machinery, since the corporation must frequently consult the Soviet user of any proposed imports, to determine his precise requirements. It is also significant that 'in many regional economic councils there are departments of external relations, which study and determine the export possibilities of the given economic region,' though the region has no right to engage directly in export deals.*

So far, the process appears to be totally unconnected with any consideration of relative prices and comparative advantage. It seems essentially quantitative, and basically this is indeed so. If an existing factory or farm in the USSR is capable of providing a particular commodity, it is unlikely in the extreme that anyone would contemplate importing it.** The problem of 'foreign competition' just will not arise and, in a planned economy, there is some logic in this. If a factory exists, and is told by the authorities to produce a thousand units of commodity A, it would not be very

*E. Kurina: *Gosudarstvennaya Monopoliya Vneshnei torgovli*, (Moscow 1959), p.7. As an exception to the general rule, some regions adjacent to foreign countries are sometimes allowed to make small barter deals.

** There are exceptions. Thus Canadian wheat has been shipped to Vladivostok to avoid burdening the Trans-Siberian railway with wheat for the Far East. Various consumers' goods (e.g. shoes from Czechoslovakia, cottons from China) do in a sense 'compete' with similar Soviet products, though the latter are insufficient to meet effective demand at existing retail prices.

sensible for another branch of the planning organs to purchase a competitive quantity of that very same commodity abroad. However, the possibility of importing a commodity can and does affect production and, above all, *investment* plans. The knowledge that rice can be bought from China, railway rolling stock from Poland, tyre factory equipment from Great Britain, would affect the planning of productive capacity. But, in making such choices, it is hard to see how the planners can take comparative advantage into account, and indeed one searches Soviet textbooks in vain for a serious analysis of the very concept of comparative advantage (as distinct from generalizations to the effect that 'the international division of labour' is a good thing).

7. *Divorce between internal and external prices*

In the practice of Soviet trade, there is a virtually complete divorce between internal and external prices. This is due partly to the nature of the internal price system, partly to a completely artificial exchange rate, and partly to the trade procedures adopted. Some reference to internal prices has already been made. The ratios of prices and costs of various commodities to one another are drastically different from those typical of 'capitalist' world markets. If Soviet prices were related to those of the West at any conceivable rate of exchange, and if decisions about imports or exports were then based on profitability and comparative cost, the result would be a drastic revision of the import plan (and the closing down of most of the Soviet textile and clothing industry) which would be quite inconsistent with the Soviet planning system. Soviet economists would argue that prices inside the USSR are adjusted to serve internal purposes, that costs in the USSR are fundamentally different to 'capitalist' costs, and that consequently it would be misleading to act on price comparisons.

Whatever may be the validity of this argument, an artificial exchange rate makes such comparisons peculiarly difficult. All trade transactions are entered in the accounts at the official rate of four roubles to the US dollar, 11.20 roubles to the pound. In principle, all goods are valued at or near 'world' (i.e. 'capitalist') prices converted at this exchange rate. For example, if wheat is sold in London at £25 per ton, it will be entered (after adjustments to bring it to f.o.b. basis) as worth $25 \times 11.20 = 280$ roubles. Similarly, a ton of wheat purchased at this price from Canada would be valued at 280 roubles.   However, in this as in nearly all other instances, the internal price level is much higher.   Thus, under the price reform of 1958, the collective farms receive from the state for grain an average price of 740 roubles per ton.   Neglecting various complications,* let us take the internal price as 740 roubles without tax. It therefore follows that the exporting corporations, having paid the producers 740 roubles, are making a big accounting loss when they sell for a nominal 280 roubles. Conversely, an importing corporation makes a large 'profit' when it resells for 740 roubles wheat bought at a nominal 280 roubles.   Of course, both the profit and the loss are an economic fiction arising from the phoney exchange rate. However, they are accounting realities.   Soviet trade corporations are reimbursed from the budget for their 'losses' in exports, or, if they both export and import, they offset 'losses' on exports against 'profits' on imports.   Importing organisations transfer the bulk of their 'profits' to the budget.   The extent of the 'profit' or 'loss' depends on the extent of the difference between Soviet internal prices and world prices.   Obviously, if the foreign trade corporations were free to choose what and when to buy or sell, they would adjust that behaviour to these differences and aim for profit maximisation. But their freedom is restricted.

8.   *How a trade corporation works*

Let us now see what one of these corporations does.   It is concerned only with the sale and/or purchase of goods on its own list.   While it can make representations about market opportunities, it is essentially charged with selling a quantity of commodities which it is told to sell.   Subject to modifications which bilateral commitments may cause, its job is then to sell for as high a price as it can get.   For example, the Exportkhleb corporation must try to get £26 and not £25 per ton of wheat if it is possible to do so, and cut its price to £24 only if the amount it has to sell cannot otherwise be disposed of. It is a fiction, which business men who deal with Russia know to be a fiction, that the corporations engage in conscious dumping, in the sense that they sell cheaper than they need.   Officials of the trade

*If 'grain' is 740 roubles per ton, wheat would be dearer.   It would also be necessary to add transportation to the port.   On the other hand, *state* farms supply wheat at a lower price than this.

corporations are rewarded for earning more foreign currency by clever bargaining and they are reprimanded if it is found that they have sold too cheaply. However, the price bears no relationship to internal prices or costs, as the example of wheat clearly shows; and on various occasions they have found it commercially desirable to reduce prices in order to sell the goods, to the dismay of those (such as the Tin Pool) who are interested in price maintenance. This has led to nonsensical stories about Red plots to disrupt capitalist markets; but, even when such nonsense is given the treatment it deserves, the fact remains that they are in a unique position of being able to sell (literally) regardless of cost, under conditions in which dumping is technically hard to prove.*

As buyers, the trade corporations strike hard bargains, and it is their duty to obtain the goods which the planners need with the least expenditure of foreign currency, subject always to bilateral commitments and other special circumstances. Among the special circumstances affecting trade policy is of course politics. The idea that Soviet trade decisions are always political in their essence is a myth. The USSR buys goods it needs and sells to pay for what it buys, and this explains the larger part of their trade. However, some important transactions can be explained only by non-economic factors, while others have a mixed motivation. Obviously, any exports which are tied in to aid programmes are as political as the aid programmes themselves. Less obviously, imports from recipients of aid are often due less to economic considerations than the necessity of accepting, in repayment of credits, whatever that particular country has to offer. Only thus can we explain the quite large Soviet imports of cashew nuts from India, to cite one example. It is also clear that a considerable portion of trade with other bloc countries is planned in advance under joint arrangements through the Council of Mutual Economic Aid (CMEA), and in these instances the trade corporations are mere technical executants of trade plans fairly precisely drawn up by planners of the countries concerned and approved by the political bosses.

These CMEA arrangements have a history of their own, which can only lightly be touched upon here. Born originally as the

---

*Or rather, it is too easy to prove. If one takes internal costs and prices at the official exchange rate, one can show that they 'dump' almost everything they sell abroad, which would be a meaningless assertion.

Soviet answer to the Marshall Plan in 1948, the CMEA led a shadowy and ineffective existence until 1956. There was in practice hardly any integration of planning, and trade was largely conducted on a bilateral and *ad hoc* basis, though expanding rapidly in volume. In the last few years, however, serious efforts have been made to dovetail long-term (15-year) plans in the Soviet orbit in Europe with those of the USSR itself*. A large number of press statements have given examples of such planning, and of the consequential trading relationships. Thus the USSR is building pipelines to supply oil to her Central European partners, and has undertaken to sell stated quantities of coal and iron ore to them in 1965, while East Germany and Czechoslovakia are to co-operate in supplying each other with the wherewithal to make and export agricultural machinery, automobiles, turbines. Poland and East Germany are to specialise in, among other things, railway rolling stock and mining equipment, and will therefore provide other Bloc members with these commodities. There are also a number of joint projects: for example, the USSR, Poland, Czechoslovakia and Roumania are collaborating in the construction of a paper and cellulose factory in the Danube delta, using local materials. They will share in the production. To some extent, therefore, the trade pattern of these countries is predetermined.

Therefore the trade corporations are by no means free to buy or sell solely with an eye to commercial advantage. They are in an anomalous position as autonomous commercial institutions, endowed with a legal personality and some appreciable range of choice in some matters, yet subject to precise direction from the politicians in others. Directions, when given, are not published, and this presents serious difficulties to anyone who seeks to understand the precise criteria on which decisions are in fact taken, or to establish whether or not there is discrimination in favour or against a particular exporting country. This causes a good deal of suspicion and is one obstacle to trade relations with a 'capitalist' economy, on which more will have to be said at a later stage.

A great deal could be written about Soviet trade policy vis-a-vis underdeveloped countries, and also on the nature and problems of

* But not with China, which stands outside this co-ordinating mechanism, though she sends an observer to CMEA meetings. For a good account of the development of CMEA, the reader is referred to Dr. A. Zauberman's article in *Problems of Communism* (Washington, D.C.), July-August 1959.

trade within the Soviet bloc. If these matters will only be lightly touched upon here, it is not because they are regarded as unimportant, but because this book is primarily concerned with East-West trade.

CHAPTER II

The Relations Between
External Trade and Internal Planning

1. *Criticism of the Soviet planning and price system*

The Soviet planning and price systems are now being subjected to strong criticism, and the search for new and more efficient methods is evidently being encouraged by the authorities. Briefly, the reasons for the search are as follows. Firstly, the sheer complexity of running a modern industrial economy is overwhelming the administrative apparatus of planning and materials allocation. Secondly, the efforts now being made to strengthen agriculture and improve housing, combined with the maintenance of a rapid growth rate in heavy industry, has made planners more conscious of the relative scarcity of resources to meet competing ends. Thirdly, there is a growing realisation that the period of relative abundance of labour is drawing to a close. Fourthly, the nature of investment has changed; instead of being concerned primarily with building new factories or installing new machines where none existed before (usually by copying western models), the problem is now one of replacing a machine by a better machine, which involves more careful assessment of relative efficiency.

Consequently, to maintain the tempo of the 'economic race' with America, the avoidance of waste, the maximization of labour productivity, the most effective use of investment resources become extremely important, and a long series of speeches, articles, books and conferences on these matters have been a feature of the Soviet scene for several years.* Outspoken criticism of the present price

* For example, Y.A. Kronrod: *Obshchestvennyi produkt pri sotsializme* (Moscow, 1958), the report of two conferences, *Zakon Stoimosti i evo rol' pri sotsializme* and *Zakon Stoimosti i evo ispolzovanie v narodnom khozyaistve* (Moscow, 1959), and numerous articles in *Voprosy Ekonomiki, Planovoe Khozyaistvo*, etc.

system and genuine argument about objective criteria for economic decisions (and especially in the field of investment choices) have appeared repeatedly in print. However, it must be admitted that the words 'foreign trade' have not been prominent in these discussions in the Soviet Union. The reason is simple: the role of foreign trade is quite small, in relation to the bulk of the Soviet economy. In 1958, Soviet exports totalled a little over 17 milliard foreign-trade roubles. In terms of internal prices, one could roughly guess that this might amount to about 30 milliards, since, as has already been pointed out, internal prices are higher than the nominal 25 US cent rouble used for trade statistics. The Soviet equivalent of our national income is not available from official sources. National income in the *Soviet* definition, which excludes non-material services, was 1,250 milliard roubles in 1958.* Adding the missing services, this would bring the total to at least 1,450 milliards, probably more. This makes exports only a shade over 2 per cent of the national income. No wonder attention is devoted primarily to internal matters. No doubt a change in the internal price and planning structure could have beneficial effects also in the field of foreign trade. However, for foreign trade to be a major cause of internal economic reforms would indeed be a case of a very small tail wagging the dog.

This is the case in the Soviet Union. But several other Communist countries are in quite a different position. On a per capita basis, Polish trade is double, Hungarian trade treble, Czech and East German trade five times, greater than the USSR.** All these countries have to import many vital materials, and are acutely conscious of the effect of balance of payments difficulties throughout the economy. Their exports are much more varied than the Russians', much more sensitive to competition and to world markets. Their economists are very conscious of the losses sustained through the absence of any proper measuring-rod of the profitability to the economy of transactions with foreign countries. Consequently, foreign trade questions have played a much bigger role in their discussions of internal economic reform. For instance, in Poland several economists have urged that internal prices of exportable commodities should reflect their full world-market prices, while

---

* Calculated from data given in *Pravda*, January 1960.

** Comparative data are cited in *Mirovaya Ekonomika i Mezhdunarodnye Otnosheniya*, No. 4/1959, p. 31.

others have been devising formulae to determine the desirability of exporting or importing a given product, in terms of the real cost of earning foreign exchange. In Hungary, trade corporations have been provided with some funds which can be invested in enterprises producing for export, thus giving them some direct power to influence the pattern of production. The Czechs too have been seeking new ways of calculating comparative advantage.

2. The value of external prices for internal planning

This is of great importance for the work of CMEA, which is supposed to be planning the long-term division of labour within the Soviet bloc. Suppose the Poles, the Czechs and the Russians are all capable of making commodity A. It is not enough to lay down a principle about the desirability of 'rational specialization within the socialist camp.' How can one tell what is rational, when the prices and costs of the three countries cannot be compared with one another? The failure to cope with the problem of relative 'socialist' prices is strikingly illustrated by use of 'world' (capitalist) prices in trade *within* the Soviet world. One eastern official, in an off-duty moment, expressed the view that, even after the world revolution, it will be necessary to preserve one capitalist country: 'otherwise how will we know at what prices to trade?' The Committees of economists and planners which sit at CMEA headquarters and argue about these problems may well have some influence on price reforms, particularly in the industrialised satellites. It is all too clear that the existing price system, and the clumsy bureaucratic centralization of trading operations, is inconsistent with a flexible and advantageous use of the 'international division of labour'.

3. The conflict between political control and freedom to trade

Attempts at reform come up against the independent centralized price-fixing of each country, and the fact that their economic life is dominated by Communist party decisions. Neither ideology nor self-interest encourages party officials to delegate their powers to anonymous economic forces. For in the last analysis, there is a choice between managers acting in accordance with orders 'transmitted' by the price mechanism, or obeying orders of a different kind passed down the party and state machine. Foreign trade officials, jealous of their monopoly, strongly oppose any extended freedom for enterprises to enter into direct commercial contact with trading partners abroad. Progress, therefore, has been slow, despite a torrent of words urging change.

4. *The use of markets in Yugoslavia*

An example of another approach may be seen in Yugoslavia. In that country, subject to controls over investment, each enterprise is very largely autonomous, though legally state-owned. There is much less price-control, and the bulk of the producing enterprises receive no production plan from above. They adjust their activities to the price and market situation, and compete with one another. The government, in principle, acts by modifying the economic incentives provided, not by direct administrative interference. This, especially in the field of foreign trade, has led to a complex and somewhat illogical system: multiple exchange rates, special foreign-currency bonuses, etc., make rational calculation difficult. But the existence of these multiple rates is in itself proof of the rights of the *enterprises* to engage in foreign trade, a right which they do not possess in the USSR.

It is true that Yugoslav enterprises have to use specialized foreign-trade agencies as intermediaries, but the agencies are numerous and compete with one another, whereas in the USSR they each have a monopoly for the given product. The wide disparity in exchange rates for exporting and importing various commodities is explained by Yugoslav economists as a temporary consequence of big disequilibria between internal and external price levels, and of an extremely critical balance-of-payments situation. It should be modified in the near future. Clearly, the system has the merit of flexibility. A Yugoslav enterprise which considers it desirable to import an item of German or French equipment knows the exchange-rate at which it can buy the necessary marks or francs, and, in principle, can order it through a trading agency without having to have it incorporated in a plan higher up the hierarchy. Although Yugoslavia and her system are regarded as ideologically 'unclean', her orthodox Communist neighbours will surely have to move in this direction under the pressures of logic and necessity. Despite various obstacles to change, one certainly should not assume that the Soviet bloc countries are inherently incapable of devising a system significantly better than the present one.

CHAPTER III

Discrimination in External Trade

1. *A consequence of the planning process*

One constant feature of trade deals between Soviet countries and the outside world, and even more of Soviet countries with each other, has been a marked tendency towards bilateralism. There are, of course, some examples of multilateralism; thus the sterling area is evidently treated as a whole, so that the Soviets use their surplus with the United Kingdom to finance purchases from the rest of the sterling area and even from some outside countries which, like Indonesia, are willing to accept sterling payments; also one sees the USSR using her dollar earnings from (for instance) sales to the United States to buy Canadian wheat or Cuban sugar. However, the fact remains that bilateral agreements are the most common form of trade deal. Why?

The answer lies primarily in the nature of the planning process, and this explains why bilateralism is particularly common *within* the Soviet bloc itself. If one relies on quantitative planning for some years ahead, it is far simpler to make an agreement with one country, or at most conclude a triangular deal. Thus the USSR may order machinery worth a certain sum from East Germany, and this can be roughly balanced by earmarking certain quantities of Russian iron ore and oil to pay for it. Discrepancies which would arise from unforeseen circumstances, or price changes, can then be taken care of by direct negotiation between the two countries. To bring in others involves complications, even if these others are also members of the Soviet bloc. There are some provisions for multi-lateral clearing between the various bloc countries, but these are little used. If 'capitalist' countries are involved, which do not

33

c

plan and are reluctant to conclude long-term agreements, it injects still greater uncertainty into the process of planning. Of course, none of these difficulties are insuperable, but considerations of sheer administrative convenience constantly encourage bilateralism. Thus the office of the Ministry of Foreign Trade which deals with the given country is happier if it can show a balance rather than a deficit which some other office would have to strive to cover. One sees this even in the activities of individual trade corporations. Thus some British business men have been dismayed to find themselves offered a kind of barter deal. This would mean that a Soviet corporation which engages in both imports and exports is trying to balance its own sterling accounts. This is a bureaucratic rather than an economic logic, but none the less real for that.

Bilateralism is clumsy and leads to unnecessary economic loss. One sees its consequences in the structure of Soviet imports, since the USSR finds itself compelled to take from (for example) Bulgaria and China various goods low in the scale of priorities, because only these are available to pay directly for Soviet exports. This is only partially modified by the re-export, notably by the USSR, of goods which she had found it convenient to over-import.* Increasingly the advantages of multilateralism are seen by economists in the Soviet bloc, particularly in the countries most dependent on trade. Yet little has been done. Part of the explanation for this state of affairs has already been given, but it should be added that the attitude of western countries is often unhelpful. One often finds western negotiators pressing for bilateral balancing, and doing their best to avoid a situation in which their eastern trading partner obtains a disposable surplus. The West in its negotiations often insists on quotas for specified goods, thereby limiting the freedom of choice of Soviet-type trade corporations, even when these would otherwise be encouraged to buy and sell on straightforward commercial lines.

The attitude of the western countries appears to contradict their belief in multilateralism, and to require some explanation. The explanation is essentially linked to the questions of Most Favoured Nation treatment (MFN) and reciprocity, and, as these points are of key importance, it is necessary to examine them more closely.

* Chinese tin and Egyptian cotton are examples of this.

2. *The attitude of the West*

The easiest way to appreciate the dilemma is to put the case of each side against the other. This involves making some attempt at understanding what the Soviet point of view is, for it is only by trying to see their problems as *they* see them that we can rationally assess their actions, present and future.

The western argument is this. If we grant a Soviet country MFN treatment, then we throw our market open to competition on normal commercial conditions, and this opportunity could be unfairly misused by the Russians, Czechs, etc., selling at prices which bear no relation to cost. But even if no dumping occurs and the competition is 'fair' (which can never be proved), the Soviet Union and its allies cannot give us reciprocal treatment, because their imports are governed by a state monopoly, which can decide what to buy, and from whom, without reference to recognisable commercial considerations. Thus the USSR buys footwear from Czechoslovakia, China and India, and not from Great Britain; it buys fish from Iceland and Norway, and hardly any from Great Britain. There may be rational reasons for this or there may not. We do not know what criteria are adopted. However, it is clear that British footwear manufacturers and fishermen (to take these two examples) are in no position to compete freely for the Soviet market. A secret memorandum from a government office can determine the course of trade. The fact that tariff duties are equal for all countries, or indeed non-existent, has no practical bearing on Soviet purchasing policy. Therefore the only way to ensure fair treatment is by limiting many Soviet exports (i.e. refusing them MFN treatment) and bargaining bilaterally for the admission of our goods to the Soviet Union, and especially of those consumers' goods which the Soviet (or Polish, or Czech) foreign traders will normally be reluctant to buy. Many West European countries take this view of the situation.

3. *The Soviet attitude*

Now let us put the contrary view. A Soviet or Czech official would argue as follows. Yes, there is indeed a difference in trading methods, but, far from being unfair to the West, it is unfair to the East. A Soviet country is in a position to sign long-term contracts which, once signed, are always firmly honoured. For example, the USSR or Poland has signed such contracts for large sums, and would sign

more if there were some assurance that they could be paid for by
Soviet or Polish exports. What assurance is there? All the West
can offer, given the system of private trade, is the *opportunity* to
sell in a highly competitive market. Yet the West, in the name of
'reciprocity', refuses to allow equal competition by refusing MFN
treatment. The Soviet countries (they argue) wish to buy to the limit
of their resources. Therefore, the more the West will take, the more
the East can buy (and, of course, vice versa.) Why is this not
reciprocity? As for the nature of the goods Soviets wish to import,
it is their business rather than ours.* It could also be said that the
Soviet corporations would buy with greater reference to purely
commercial considerations if their hands were not tied by bilateral
commitments insisted on by western negotiators, because it is
financially advantageous to them to buy in the cheapest market.

Both positions have some basis in logic and fact. Part of the problem facing each western country in isolation is that it may be ousted
by other western countries who may insist on bilateral quotas; for
example, if France bargains for a quota of clothing exports to
Roumania and the British Board of Trade fails to negotiate one too,
it is open to attack from the clothing industry for failing to do its
duty. Then, again, if *one* western country freely admits goods from
the East which other western countries restrict, it is liable to find
its market flooded, whereas, since export surpluses of the East are
generally somewhat limited, the danger of 'flooding' would be
much less if all western markets were open. There is much to be said,
therefore, for a common policy on the part of the West, designed to
encourage any tendency towards a more 'commercial' approach
to trade on the part of the East. This does not dispose of the danger
of dumping (however motivated), but perhaps this danger could be
eliminated by the existence of reserve powers to impose restrictions.
The danger of restrictions cannot help but influence the behaviour
of eastern trade corporations; as one of their chiefs put it, 'we do
not get a bonus if, by our price policy, we cause the imposition of an
anti-dumping duty'. It should be possible to arrive at some less
negative solution, which would facilitate rather than hinder the
expansion of trade, which would combine the granting of selling

* It has become almost traditional for British and other western negotiators
to insist on consumers' goods quotas. One wonders why. Does it really
matter to us whether the Russians buy a lathe or a carpet with their money,
unless, of course, we lack the productive capacity to meet their orders for lathes?

opportunities with safeguards against possible disorganization of the market.

Some new thinking on reciprocity and multilateralism would therefore not come amiss, in the West as well as in the East. In this connection, the deal negotiated by the De Beers diamond interests and the USSR is of very great interest. Instead of stubbornly endeavouring to keep a growing Soviet industry out of world markets, it may pay western business men to offer (where this is organizationally possible) a limited share under proper safeguards. One wonders whether or when the oil companies will do the same.

CHAPTER IV

The Limitations on External Trade

1. *Shortage of means of payment*

In seeking to assess the principal bottlenecks, or limiting factors, which stand in the way of a large expansion of trade with the Soviet bloc, it is necessary to consider first of all the shortage of means of payment on the Soviet side. Now that the deliberate restriction of all contacts with foreigners, typical of the late-Stalin period, is a thing of the past, and trade expansion is regarded by Soviet leaders as politically a good thing, it seems a realistic assumption to take the import needs of the Soviet bloc as, for all practical purposes, infinite. By this is meant the fact that the demand for imports, expressed in terms of requests for import authorization, very greatly exceeds the possibility of paying for such imports. This is, of course, a generalization valid in aggregate terms only. It would not apply (for example) to exports of shoes to Czechoslovakia, railway wagons to Poland or furs to the USSR, since the countries in question have large surpluses of these products. But there is abundant evidence that import plans have to be cut to fit payments possibilities. This evidence is, as might be expected, most striking in the countries of eastern Europe. Thus Polish economists and planners make no secret of their belief that foreign exchange earnings severely limit not only their imports but also the expansion of the entire economy. It goes without saying that, if means of payment *were* freely available, imports would be restricted by other considerations, such as protection of home industries or the desire to ensure economic-strategic independence. However, these considerations do not operate as effective limiting factors in the short run.

39

2. *The urge to autarky*

Why, then, cannot the Soviet Union and its allies expand their sales substantially, and thereby earn more means of payment? Part of the answer is that they are doing so, and indeed the volume of their sales has been rising, as is clear from the statistics. However, several obstacles stand in the way of very rapid expansion. Firstly there is the habit of autarky, which has already been commented on. If goods are short, the first thought of a planner is to produce them at home, or alternatively to give priority to a source within the Soviet bloc, which can be 'tied up' with long-term agreements and/or joint planning arrangements. If they are in surplus, the surplus quantities can be made available for export, but the investment plan is unlikely to provide for rapid expansion of the commodity in surplus. This generalization has many exceptions and applies much more to the USSR (and probably to China too) than to Poland, or Czecho-slovakia.* However, it has some validity. Planners always face more demands on investment funds than the resources available. Consequently applications for investment have to be cut, and it is the natural tendency of planners to direct scarce investment resources to cope with actual or anticipated shortages within the country, rather than to provide capacity for possible sales to uncertain 'capitalist' markets. Surpluses often bear a chance character, and vary greatly from year to year. For example, the USSR has had a sizeable surplus of pig-iron and aluminium, and of wheat in good harvest years, but it is quite possible that internal requirements could at any time absorb all the home output of these commodities; thus the Soviets' own plans envisage a rise in the domestic utilization of these and other commodities, which can only to a limited extent be varied by substituting other materials or cutting non-priority uses. In the case of timber, a traditional export and a vital source of sterling, exports are maintained despite abundant evidence of shortages inside the USSR itself. A balance has to be struck between the intensity of internal need and the urgency of the import for which payment is required.

3. *Unhelpfulness from the West?*

The Soviet Union and (particularly) its allies are becoming in-

---

* Thus Poland offers export goods in short supply at home, giving exports a high priority.

creasingly aware of the need to provide additional export surpluses. But another obstacle must now be mentioned; the reluctance of western trading partners to take some goods which the USSR and its allies can offer.   Two examples, affecting this country, are Soviet oil and Polish bacon.   Obviously, it is of no use for the Poles to expand their bacon production for export when even their present offerings are considered to be too much for the British market, while most other western markets are even less 'hospitable'.   Nor would an enlarged Soviet surplus of aluminium be welcomed with open arms in the western world.

Again, western policies in these matters have some reasons behind them, yet the consequences are not altogether logically thought out.   Far too often, western exporters expect the Soviets to expand their purchases without realizing that no large expansion of Soviet buying is possible unless we take many more of their goods. Similarly, people speak optimistically about the vast potential of China as a market, but hardly ever consider that this involves a big expansion in Chinese competition in the sterling area and world markets generally, though it should be obvious enough.   While it is true that the Russians can finance deficits with gold sales to some extent (more about gold in a moment), their allies produce no gold and must pay for what they buy in goods.   It could be argued that they could cover a deficit with one western country by earning a surplus with another, but, as we have seen, they are seldom permitted to earn a surplus, so the argument is somewhat theoretical.   On present evidence, it could well be maintained that the *immediate* bottleneck is not shortage of exportable surpluses on the Soviet side but import restrictions on the western side—though, if these restrictions did not exist, the eastern countries would rapidly find that they have not enough goods with which to take full advantage of their opportunities.

What is the *rationale* behind western restrictions?   The argument about MFN and reciprocity has been given already, but it is far from being the whole story. There is a genuine difficulty which faces many western governments and business men.   The export effort of the Soviet bloc is inevitably concentrated in a comparatively narrow range of commodities, for which the market is limited.   Any big rise in offerings from a new source is liable to hurt other producers, and may force prices down.   Of course, from a traditional liberal-economic standpoint this can only be beneficial: thus Britain's terms of trade would improve if Soviet exports cause a reduction in the prices at which we buy raw materials.

However, things are seldom so simple. All kinds of obstacles arise. For instance, there are various international commodity arrangements, such as the wheat agreement, which limit our freedom of action. The troubles which arose when Soviet supplies threatened established tin and aluminium interests are fresh in the memory. Large arrivals of Polish bacon would lead to acute difficulties with home producers and with the Danes. The special position of the oil companies, their price maintenance arrangements, their agreements to divide world markets, are inconsistent with the admission of large quantities of Soviet oil. The list can be prolonged. Faced with these problems, it is by no means obvious that the western governments should be blamed for, in effect, giving preference to their links with non-Soviet countries. For example, British connections with Australia (or West Germany's with Italy, and so on) seem not only politically but also economically more durable and reliable, compared with their relations with Soviet countries. Consequently, when the Australians (or whoever it may be) complain that competition from a Soviet source is depriving them of export earnings, and perhaps compelling them to restrict their imports, it is hardly surprising that any British government hearkens to the complaints, in the long-term interest of British business. For it remains true that trade with the USSR or Czechoslovakia is more hazardous, more likely to be interrupted by political difficulties, or sudden and unforeseeable changes in planning decisions, than is trade with the Commonwealth or our European neighbours.

Consequently, even though we may believe that the expansion of East-West trade is politically desirable (which we discuss below), there are economic grounds for avoiding excessive damage to the interests of our traditional trading associates and to various international commodity agreements which (presumably) we have had good reason for joining, or for ourselves becoming too dependent on exports to Soviet bloc countries. This does not mean that our present policies in these respects are always wise, or that it would not be in our interests to admit more Soviet goods in order to facilitate mutually-advantageous trade. Indeed, we may find that the net effect is also to benefit our traditional customers. For example,

if the Soviets sell more in the United Kingdom and use the extra
sterling to buy more rubber and wool in the sterling area, the Commonwealth producers should have (on balance) no grounds for
complaint. Nor is there any danger of our economy becoming over-
dependent on Russian trade: only a tiny fraction of British trade is,
or is likely to be, with the Soviet world: thus British exports to the
USSR in 1958 were well below 1 per cent of total exports. Then, of
course, it should be clear that Soviet exports which are kept out of
our market will probably appear elsewhere; thus Soviet oil which we
refuse to buy may compete with British oil companies in third
countries. The problem is one of striking a rational balance between
all the various interests involved, and no one can pretend that this
is an easy task.

4. *The strategic controls*

The Soviet Union and its allies used to complain bitterly about the
'strategic controls' which deprived them of a wide range of goods
they wished to import. These complaints have been much reduced
in volume since the revision of the list of controlled goods. Few
business men would deny that the original list was unreasonable,
and even the present one contains items for which it is hard to find
justification, except in terms of a 'trading with the enemy' approach
which logically leads to no trade at all. However, the range of
prohibited exports is not now a major bar to the expansion of trade,
and no one pretends otherwise. More serious is the wider American
interpretation of the word 'strategic', which causes the US
authorities not only to embargo a much wider range of goods than
western European countries embargo, but also to encourage US
firms to refuse permission to firms in other countries to export
goods or processes containing American-owned patents. This is
part of a genuine difference of outlook on trade with the East, to
which further references will be made. It also shows itself in the
discrimination, in tariff duties, to which goods of Soviet bloc origin
are often subject on entry into the United States.

Given that it is ability to pay, rather than any 'strategic' restrictions
on western exports, which are the immediate limiting factor on
Soviet buying, there arise the twin questions of credits and gold sales.

5. *The role of credits*

Credits, by definition, have to be repaid. Therefore a request for credits from the Soviet side presupposes an immediate need for imports, or placing of orders, for which it is impossible to pay out of current earnings, but which it is thought will be easier to pay for at a later date. The USSR, for example, has balanced its external accounts in the last five years with the help of sizeable gold sales; but the needs of the current seven-year plan call for large purchases of equipment and know-how in advanced western countries, particularly for the relatively backward chemical industry. There is little immediate opportunity to expand exports sufficiently. In the longer run, no doubt, it is hoped to achieve the necessary expansion and thereby repay the credits.

Soviet desires in this matter are quite understandable. Western reactions are more mixed. The problem is not one of credit-worthiness. No one denies that the Soviet record in respect of commercial payments has been very good. Three objections may be raised. The first is that many western countries, and notably Great Britain, have only limited resources to invest, that many urgent projects in the Commonwealth and elsewhere call for capital, and that consequently it is undesirable to commit large sums in what would amount to a long or medium-term loan to the Soviet Union. Secondly, the granting of a large credit would logically entail admitting many more Soviet goods to enable them to repay it, which would perhaps lead to the difficulties already discussed. The third objection is more directly political: credits to the USSR strengthen their economy and therefore help them to compete with us politically. This argument I believe to be wrongheaded; it will be dealt with later along with other political objections to the development of East-West trade.

6. *Moscow gold*

Cannot the credits be repaid in gold, or cannot the goods be paid for in gold, thereby obviating the need for credits? Two things must be emphasised in this connection. One is that the Soviets already sell gold in very considerable quantities, roughly $200 million a year or more. The other is that we have no idea of the level of Soviet gold production or stocks, because the figures are secret and have been secret for many years. Western estimates about present output are purely and entirely guesswork. The secrecy is *not* proof that the total is very high. It may, on the contrary, be quite consistent with falling output. No evidence exists to disprove the assertion that current sales have been fully up to current production. The goldfields are mainly located in remote northern areas of Siberia, and used to be worked by forced labour: much of this labour force has been dispersed by successive amnesties, and their replacements have to be paid high Arctic wage rates. Costs of production are probably uneconomically high, though some methods used to calculate them cannot stand serious examination. Given the present price of gold and the relative costs of possible exportable commodities, it may well appear to Soviet planners that gold is not the best way out, or that forward planning should be based on balancing payments through trade, using gold as an emergency reserve. This view has the merit of being wholly consistent with Soviet behaviour.

7. *The prospect for rouble convertibility*

The Soviet gold reserves *may* be used, in the near future, to form the basis of rouble convertibility. Rumours to that effect have appeared in the financial press, and some (the *New York Herald-Tribune*, for instance) promptly dubbed this as 'propaganda'. It is not clear why. Of course, there is something to be made of a slogan about the rouble looking the dollar in the face. There has been a good example of a *purely* propagandist currency measure: the Soviets' upwards revaluation of the official rouble exchange rate in 1950, which had no economic rhyme or reason whatsoever. However, propaganda is not the essence of the present problem. Rouble convertibility, backed by gold, would mean that western countries earning a surplus with the USSR could rely on being able to convert it into other western currencies or into gold. Such a step would be a *sine qua non* of the development of multilateral trade, and may be intended to encourage it. Naturally, any such convertibility measures would not affect Soviet citizens in their personal capacity, or the state monopoly of foreign trade. None the less, it would neither be meaningless nor, surely, merely or mainly propaganda—if it happened. It has not happened yet.

CHAPTER V

The Prospect for Increased External Trade

1. The shortage of capital goods for the underdeveloped countries

Are we due to face a vast trade offensive from the Soviet bloc of countries which, even if prevented from penetrating into the economies of western industrialised countries, will sweep all before it in the underdeveloped and uncommitted world? If an export drive is to be feared, what could it consist of?

Answers to such questions must of necessity be somewhat speculative. Involved in them is an estimate of political intention. How much priority would the Soviet leaders give to developing trade, or granting aid, as distinct from concentrating resources on internal growth? The underdeveloped countries are particularly interested in capital goods, notably machinery. The USSR is still a net importer of machinery, and her exports go very largely to China, presumably for reasons at least as much political as economic. The growing output of machinery in East Germany and Czechoslovakia is at present heavily engaged in supplying the USSR (to a lesser extent also China, and such underdeveloped Soviet-bloc countries as Bulgaria). The long term co-ordination of trade and investment within the bloc involves the earmarking of present and future productive capacity for the needs of the bloc. It is likely that even the relatively modest exports of capital goods to non-Soviet countries cause a strain on resources that are already stretched.

This is a point to bear in mind when assessing Soviet aid-giving capacity. The capacity in question is not in essence financial: the aid takes the form of deliveries of *goods*, mainly capital goods, on credit. The availability of these goods is thus a limiting factor. It is true that a political decision can divert machinery from internal to external use. It is also true that some such decisions (for instance the Aswan dam aid project, or the Bhilai steel mill) have been taken. However, those who imagine that the Soviet top leadership give very high priority in their thinking to foreign economic adventures seem likely, on the evidence, to find themselves mistaken. Thus the 21st Party congress (February 1959) and the central committee plenum of June 1959 were both almost wholly devoted to economic, especially industrial, questions, and the hundreds of pages of verbatim reports included frank discussions of real problems facing the economy. Yet questions of foreign relations, or of foreign aid, were hardly mentioned. The only references to such questions at the June plenum were significantly concerned with the internal operations of the Soviet economy: in one instance, Khrushchev deplored the inefficient utilization of imported machinery, in another the speed of construction of the Bhilai steel mill was contrasted with the slowness with which Soviet steelworks were completed. The speeches showed a marked concentration on problems of the USSR's own growth. The seven-year plan document is the same. *Per contra*, it contains numerous ambitious internal projects to which the bulk of Soviet resources will have to be devoted.

2. *The need for imports*

However, Soviet plans do involve increased imports from non-Soviet countries, as we have seen. Therefore, quite apart from politics, they must call for higher exports. But will this last? Some critics have argued that this higher demand for imports is a temporary phenomenon, that the USSR will seek to achieve greater economic independence at the earliest date. They point to the large Soviet machinery imports of the first five-year plan period (1929-1933) which was followed by a sharp reduction. Thus the Soviet chemical industry, once modernized, will no longer need imported machines. Clearly, if the policy of import expansion is temporary, it would be dangerous for us to rely on the Soviet market, and Soviet export offerings will also be temporary (and therefore disorganizing) in character.

This view appears to me to be mistaken. The conditions of 1929-33 were very different, the drive for self-sufficiency more urgent, and greatly stimulated later in the 'thirties by the rise of Hitler and the threat of war. It is, of course, true that self-sufficiency in a basic, 'strategic' sense is and will be an aim of Soviet policy; thus they would not allow themselves to be dependent on the West for their supplies of (say) electronic equipment. Much naturally depends on the international climate, but there does seem ample long-term scope for trade; when the purchases of chemical machinery are completed, no doubt they will turn to other things which the West has developed better. The campaign for a rapid expansion of the chemical industry will certainly not be the last campaign to expand a backward sector. One can draw up a long catalogue of industries in the USSR which could be re-equipped with advantage with good western machines: some obvious examples are the antique and inefficient clothing industry, furniture-making and food-processing; others include a range of textile machinery, materials moving equipment, computors, newspaper presses, mass-production equipment and know-how for making a variety of consumers' goods which are still produced in fairly primitive workshops. The list will doubtless grow, as the West is not standing still.

In addition to its demands for machinery, the rapid growth of the economy must lead to increased requirements of many kinds of materials which cannot be produced in sufficient quantities within the USSR. Many such already appear in Table II B (on page 93) and others will join them. East Germany, Czechoslovakia and Poland, which rely more than the Soviet Union on imported materials, will probably need greatly increased quantities also. Apart from considerations of sheer physical scarcity, the new consciousness of the importance of counting the cost may also cause the Soviets to import 'capitalist' goods in order to save transport. The USSR is vast, overland distances are enormous, and, just as Canadian wheat has been sent to Vladivostok, and Polish coal to the Baltic coast, other bulky commodities may find their way to other Soviet ports remote from internal sources of supply. The same might come to influence the import policy of the Czechs and the East Germans; it is not always logical to rely on Soviet materials, if these need to be hauled several thousand miles by rail.

Nor should we neglect the inexhaustible demand for consumers' goods. Table II B shows that a range of foodstuffs, clothing and other such goods are imported already. It is true that these come largely from within the bloc, but there is no ideological principle to

D

prevent their being bought from other countries; the available 'hard currency' has so far been earmarked for priority purchases of raw materials and capital goods; it need not always be so, if shortages of materials and of currency become less acute. Thus the potentialities for expansion are there, even though, for reasons repeatedly referred to in these pages, its extent may be more modest than some of the more sanguine commentators expect. No doubt our sales to the east can be increased by quite impressive percentages. But let us not forget that, even if they are trebled, sales to all the Soviet bloc would amount to a bare 9 per cent of British exports. The belief that East-West trade is a cure-all for our economic difficulties is a myth.

In earlier pages we have insisted on the limitations imposed by lack of Soviet exportable surpluses. There seems every ground for expecting a rise in their import requirements. Therefore, their planners will have, somehow or other, to make more goods available for export.

3. *Exports from the East*

Let us first take the USSR. There are certain definite possibilities of expansion. Oil is clearly one of them; the USSR is extending pipelines into Central Europe, and building more tankers, and planned expansion may well significantly outstrip the rise in internal demand, since oil production is to double in the period 1958-65, representing an *annual* rate of increase of 17 million tons. Then the plans are known to provide for a very large expansion in iron ore exports to the Soviet bloc.* There may well be more available for the outside world. Steel production is likely to be wholly absorbed by domestic needs, but there are possibilities of rapid and low-cost expansion of the aluminium industry in Siberia. If reports of rich finds in the Yakut region are correct, there may be a sizeable export trade in diamonds before many years are out. When the re-equipment of Soviet agriculture is further advanced, there may be surplus capacity, available for export, in the tractor and other farm machinery industries. Some other well-developed engineering sectors (perhaps machine-tools, or excavators) could provide a surplus, but the whole

* Sales of iron ore to Czechoslovakia alone are to increase from 3·6 million tons in 1958 to 10·1 million tons in 1965 (*Mirovaya Ekonomika i Mezhdunarodnye Otnosheniya*. No. 4/1959. p. 28.)

question of machinery exports is bound up with uncertainties about internal requirements and China's needs. Motor car output, actual and planned, is so moderate* as to present no serious menace, save perhaps in some one small market. Traditional items like grain and timber are doubtless intended to expand, but here too there is a rapid rise in the USSR's own requirements with which to contend. It is possible that, with the help of their new atomic icebreaker, the Soviets intend to open up a new way to the vast forests of Siberia; the present shortage of timber in Russia is due to transportation difficulties rather than shortage of trees. As for grain, the plans provide for a large rise in output, harvests tend to vary greatly from year to year, and export offerings vary also, as may be observed from the figures in Table II B. Given the peculiarities of the Russian climate, and the relative inelasticity of internal demand, such variations are likely to continue also in the future.**

Other commodities may be offered in years in which supply happens to outstrip demand: pig-iron, raw cotton, various metals, flax, may appear and disappear in world markets. Some mass-produced consumer durables, for instance watches and radios, may be sold in increasing quantities with the relative saturation of the internal market.

The Czechs and the East Germans have a rapidly-developing engineering industry, and it is virtually certain that their competition will be increasingly felt in Latin America, Asia and elsewhere, though, as already mentioned, Soviet and Chinese demands may pre-empt much of the available supplies.

4. China

This leaves China. It must be admitted that, while the whole of this rough survey of prospects bristles with uncertainties, the behaviour

---

* Total Soviet production in 1958 of *all* motor vehicles was only about 500,000.

** It is true that the seven-year plan provides for a very large increase (by 8 per cent per annum) in agricultural production, and for a grain harvest of 164-180 million tons, which would mean an increase of some 50 per cent over the 1954-8 average (the 1958 harvest of 141 million tons was an all-time record, and the 1959 figure was down to 124·8). However, Soviet history shows that agricultural, unlike industrial, plans are seldom fulfilled. Undeniably there has been an impressive recovery in agricultural output from the low levels of 1949-53, and some increases must be expected also in the future. However, if the promised improvements in living and nutritional standards are to be translated into reality, domestic consumption must be expected to absorb any likely rise in production.

of Chinese traders is even more completely a matter of speculation. At present China's trade is overwhelmingly within the Soviet bloc. This may be a matter of ideological preference. It may even more be due to sheer necessity: the West has been reluctant, especially in the Korean war period, to expand trade, and to this day the United States imposes a complete boycott. Negotiations with Japan about expansion of trade have so far largely foundered on political rocks of mutual suspicion. In any case, China is in a difficult position. The enormously ambitious plans for internal development ('the great leap forward') have brought with them overcommitment of resources, transport bottlenecks and a good deal of sheer confusion.* This had the simultaneous effect of greatly adding to import demand, while disorganising the output and movement of export commodities. One must suppose that the confusion will not last long. But, even with order restored, exportable surpluses will be hard to find, and these are already being largely used to pay the Soviet bloc countries for the capital equipment and the oil which China needs for her industrial growth. For reasons of political prestige, China has even granted some aid to certain non-bloc countries (Ceylon, Cambodia), as well as helping North Viet-Nam and North Korea. At present, *total* Chinese trade is very modest indeed for a country of well over 600 million people: exports in 1957 were worth a mere $2,200 million, or very much below those of the Netherlands. Over a third of this went to the Soviet Union, and much of the rest to other 'Soviet' countries.**

China's present situation seems similar to that of the USSR thirty years ago, when she too was engaged in a 'crash' programme of rapid industrialization from small beginnings. When opportunities are found to buy more of the sinews of industrialization from 'capitalist' countries, the Chinese authorities will doubtless throw on the world market whatever can be found to pay for these imports, even though (as in Russia in 1930-33) the internal market goes very short. The traditional Chinese bristles, preserved eggs and tung oil would be a drop in the ocean. Already, to pay for needed materials from south-east Asia, the Chinese have had to export manufactures

*The drastic downward revision of the 1959 plan, and 'correction' of the statistical claims for 1958, which were published in the Chinese press in August 1959, show both over-ambitious planning and pure muddle.

** Figures are taken from an unpublished draft article by E. Szczepanik, of the University of Hong Kong, by kind permission of its author.

(especially textiles) to these countries at prices which markedly undercut even Japan. China exports vast quantities of rice, oilseeds, fruit and even footwear to the USSR, and no doubt could sell more of such things, provided domestic production can satisfy even the minimum demands of a population increasing at the rate of 13 millions a year.

In the case of China, so much depends on politics, including internal 'economic' politics, that any attempt at a forecast can be quite exceptionally wide of the mark. Demand is potentially colossal, and extends over a vast range of capital goods and many raw materials, but no wise business man would wish to put all his eggs into this basket.

CHAPTER VI

A Politico-Economic Appraisal

Is the expansion of East-West trade in our interests? Or should we reduce it to a minimum? Such questions do in fact underlie many differences of policy between Britain and America, and are worth looking at from the broadest political-economic viewpoint.

1. *The American view*

Again, it would be a help to clarity if the two arguments were plainly stated. The view common in America may be summarized as follows. The USSR and its fellow-countries are engaged in a world-wide struggle to defeat the West. Even allowing that Khrushchev's desire to 'bury' America is non-military in its essence, it does mean that he and his allies are planning to oust the United States and its allies by economic means plus 'peaceful' forms of subversion. The seven year plan is part of this campaign for world domination; like most other Soviet economic measures, it is related more or less directly to the overriding goal of Soviet policy: our overthrow. It follows that we should do nothing to help. The criterion of whether trade should or should not take place is therefore the importance of the proposed imports to the fulfilment of the plans of the Soviet bloc. The more useful the commodity is to them, the more they should be deprived of it. Certainly every priority should be given, in imports and in exports, to deals with non-Soviet countries ('the Free World')*. It is not just a matter of directly 'strategic' (i.e. military) goods. Anything which makes their economy more efficient, even plastics for handbags, adds to their menace, if only by

* Portugal? Spain? The Dominican Republic? Saudi Arabia? Perhaps we need a new term.

releasing resources which could then be used for nefarious purposes. Credits are anathema, because they help the Soviets to fulfil their plan more quickly and easily.

This is a not unfair rendering of the views of, among others, Assistant Secretary of State Dillon.

2. *The counter-arguments*

The counter-arguments should, if seriously meant, go a little deeper than mere commercial advantage. It would be undignified as well as pitiful to accept the premises and say: 'we need the money'. The points to make are, surely, these. Firstly, we should not accept the view that the Soviets must always be fully occupied with plotting our downfall. Already they are much more concerned with their *internal* growth than their critics allow. Their hostile acts towards us may be, often are, influenced by our acts towards them. Trade establishes *mutually* advantageous relations. It strengthens the USSR, true, but it also strengthens us. Were it otherwise, neither side would trade at all. The logic of the American position is total boycott, such as they impose on trade with China. Trade relations make both sides more dependent on each other, and enlarge points of contact. This is why Stalin tried to reduce such relations; surely we ought not to follow Stalin's policy *à l'envers*. Above all, it is an indefensible position to take up in public. Opinion, in this country, and still more in uncommitted states, would not understand a policy which sought to obstruct normal commercial exchanges. It ill behoves us to act as if we feared trade contacts, or preferred two autarkic world blocs. We cannot criticise the Soviet countries for not acting on rational commercial lines in their trade and investment policies, and then cut off supplies to them because of the urgency of their need for a given set of goods. This is particularly illogical politically in the case of the European satellites, many of whom appear to be genuinely desirous of becoming less dependent on the Soviet Union economically. All the foregoing applies equally to credits. A commercial credit, voluntarily granted at the market rate of interest, is not aid, but a normal commercial transaction; all that happens is that one is paid (somewhat more) in a few years' time. Unless one seriously supposes that an all-out clash is due within these years, credits should be no more barred on *political* grounds than any other transaction.

3. *A reason for hope*

Let us remember that it is over forty years since the Russian revolution. It would be strange indeed if the original missionary faith still animates the Soviet leadership, whatever they may say in the ideological passages of their speeches. Their country is becoming richer, more and more Soviet citizens, and especially in the official, technological and intellectual classes, have possessions, a stake in the country, a wish for stability. Even the more enthusiastic Soviet ideologists should have drawn cautious conclusions from the danger of an H-bomb age. We have grounds for hoping for a lessening of revolutionary dynamic among the Soviet ruling groups. One of the factors which maintains this dynamic is the belief that the outside world is implacably hostile. This is what the textbooks of Marxism-Leninism tell them, and this is what a 'blockade' approach to trading relations would help to confirm. In any case, the negative approach is essentially defeatist.

Why should every exchange between East and West work out to their advantage? Do we really think that the eastern bloc would win the economic 'competition', would really 'bury' us, if we traded with them on a normal commercial basis? Of course, this involves selling them the goods they want to pursue their economic programmes; what other basis is there for trade? We cannot consider ourselves doomed by the forces of history in which Khrushchev claims to have such faith. In any economic competition we start with formidable advantages. Closer relations may give them opportunities, but they give us opportunities too. If it makes them richer, so much the better. Dangerous men, like Cassius, have a lean and hungry look.

I realise that this view can be disputed. There is, indeed, no *assurance* that greater material prosperity will make Soviet communism easier to live with. It is certainly arguable that a well-fed Bolshevik is no whit less dangerous than a hungry Bolshevik—assuming he remains the same kind of Bolshevik; but will he?

Book I

Part II

The Economic Structure
of Communist Countries

The Economic Structure of Communist Countries

A. THE 104 ECONOMIC ADMINISTRATIVE REGIONS ('SOVNARKHOZY') OF THE UNION OF SOVIET SOCIALIST REPUBLICS

The notes list the capital city, area, population and main industries of each region. Where the capital is not named, it bears the same name as the region. Population data refer to the last census, January 1959. Percentages giving the relative importance of industries within a region relate to 1957 or 1958, or as otherwise stated.

There are 15 Soviet Socialist Republics:

A	Russian Soviet Socialist Republic		(68 Sovnarkhozy)	
B	Ukrainian Soviet Socialist Republic		(11	ditto)
C	Kazakhstan	ditto	(9	,,)
D	Uzbekistan	,,	(5	,,)
E	Azerbaidzjan	,,	(one Sovnarkhoz)	
F	Armenian	,,	(one	,,)
G	Byelorussian	,,	(one	,,)
H	Georgian	,,	(one	,,)
I	Kirghizian	,,	(one	,,)
J	Latvian	,,	(one	,,)
K	Lithuanian	,,	(one	,,)
L	Moldavian	,,	(one	,,)
M	Tadjik	,,	(one	,,)
N	Turkmen	,,	(one	,,)
O	Estonian	,,	(one	,,)

A. RUSSIAN SOVIET SOCIALIST REPUBLIC. Capital: Moscow. 17,076,900 sq. km. 117,494,000 inhabitants (52 per cent urban).

The gross industrial output of Russia accounts for about 63.8 per cent of the USSR total. It is divided into 68 Sovnarkhozy.

1. ALTAI. Capital: Barnaul. 261,600 sq. km. 2,685,000 inhabitants (33 per cent urban). Metalworking and engineering (60 per cent of gross industrial output of Altai in 1948), food processing industry (cheese—first in the USSR, sugar, fats), textiles (cotton fabrics), chemicals (based on the rich resources of salt), timber, wood processing, mining (gold, precious metals and semi-precious stones) and electricity generating industry. Predominantly agricultural region.

2. AMUR. Capital: Blagoveshchensk. 363,700 sq. km. 717,000 inhabitants (60 per cent urban). Over 50 per cent of the area is covered by forests. Timber and wood processing (employing in 1956 about 22 per cent of the total industrial labour force), gold mining (about 16.4 per cent), engineering and metalworking (11 per cent), coal mining (7.7 per cent) and non-ferrous metals.

3. ARKHANGELSK. 594,200 sq. km. 1,278,000 inhabitants (53 per cent urban). Timber and wood processing, based on very rich resources of high-quality wood, shipbuilding, mining (gypsum, non-ferrous metals, coal, peat), food processing (fish, fat), some engineering (transport equipment), furs, etc.

4. ASTRAKHAN. 44,100 sq. km. 702,000 inhabitants (52 per cent urban). Fishing and fish processing, salt extracting (30 per cent of the USSR production in 1950), ship-building (fishing boats), wood processing, building materials (gypsum), food processing (fish, fat, fruit), chemicals and paper.

5. BASHKIRIA. Capital: Ufa. 143,600 sq. km. 3,335,000 inhabitants (38 per cent urban). Oil (in 1956 first in the USSR), metalworking (steel, rolling mill products), mining (coal, non-ferrous metals), timber and wood processing (plywood), food processing (meat, sugar), light industries (woollen fabrics, clothing, leather footwear, leather), chemicals, building materials, and gas. 50 per cent of surface area is covered by forests.

6. BELGOROD. 27,100 sq. km. 1,227,000 inhabitants (only 18 per cent urban). Small industries include chalk processing, clothing, building materials (bricks), food-processing (tinned food, flour, beer, bread, etc.), growing importance of iron ore mining.

7. BRYANSK. 34,900 sq. km. 1, 547,000 inhabitants (35 per cent urban). Engineering and metalworking (in 1956 employed 30 per cent of the total industrial labour force) producing wagons, steam locomotives, agricultural machinery, etc.; also paper, timber and wood-processing (19 per cent), light industries 18 per cent (clothing, silk, jute, leather footwear), food processing 11 per cent (flour, bread, vegetables and alcohol), fuel 6 per cent (peat), building materials 6 per cent (cement, glass) and electricity generation (using peat).

8. BURYAT.   Capital: Ulan-Ude. 351,200 sq. km. 671,000 inhabitants (41 per cent urban). Metalworking and engineering, mining of coal, shale, gold, electricity generating, timber, glass, some textiles (woollen fabrics), and fishing and fish-processing (Baikal lake). Metalworking and engineering industries accounted for about 45 per cent of the total gross industrial output.

9. VLADIMIR. 28,902 sq. km., 1,402,000 inhabitants (57 per cent urban). Textiles (employing about 33.7 per cent of the total industrial labour force and producing cotton, linen, etc.), engineering and metalworking 32 per cent (television sets, motor-cycles, tractors, excavators, etc.), timber and wood processing (8.1 per cent-42 per cent of area covered by forests), glass 7.6 per cent (crystal glass). Minor industries include food processing 4.1 per cent (meat, fish, fat, flour, macaroni, etc.), clothing (3.8 per cent), fuel 3.4 per cent (peat), production of building materials and electricity generating.

10. VOLOGDA. 145,500 sq. km. 1,307,000 inhabitants (35 per cent urban). Timber and wood processing industry (accounts for about 30 per cent of the total gross industrial output and produces sawn-wood, plywood, furniture, cellulose and paper). Other industries are food processing (animal and vegetable oil), textile (linen), engineering (machinery for wood processing industry and agriculture, transport equipment), glass and power generating industry (peat).

11. VORONEZH. 63,400 sq. km. 2,363,000 inhabitants. (35 per cent urban). Principally agricultural area.   Main industries are metallurgy (based on the locally produced iron-ore), engineering producing miscellaneous machinery, tractors, excavators and cranes), building materials (cement, glass, gypsum, bricks), chemicals (pharmaceutical products, synthetic rubber products such as tyres,

footwear etc.), food-processing (food extracts, fat), and other light industries.

12. GORKI. 73,200 sq. km. 3,590,000 inhabitants (52 per cent urban). One of the most important industrial regions of the USSR The most important industries are engineering notably automobiles, (one of the biggest factories in Europe), construction equipment etc. Engineering industry accounts for about 70 per cent of the total gross industrial output. Other important industries are electricity generation (peat and water resources of the river Volga), metallurgy, timber, paper, glass, chemicals (processing wood), light industries (knitwear, clothing, footwear), food processing (macaroni, confectionery, dairy-products) and oil refining.

13. DAGESTAN. Capital: Makhachkala. 50,300 sq. km. 1,063,000 inhabitants (30 per cent urban). The most important industries are engineering and metal-working (in 1950 accounted for about 56 per cent of the gross industrial output), food processing 18 per cent (meat, tinned food, cheese, confectionery), also some oil extracting and natural gas (about 3 per cent), textiles (3.6 per cent), building materials 2.6 per cent (bricks, cement, tiles, glass), electricity generation and fishing on the Caspian Sea.

14. IVANOVO. 24,000 sq. km. 1,306,000 inhabitants (66 per cent urban). Its main industries are textiles (employing about 65 per cent of the total industrial labour force), clothing (7.3 per cent), engineering and metalworking (6.6 per cent), timber and wood processing (3.2 per cent), food processing (3.1 per cent producing meat, fat, processed fish etc.), peat mining (3.5 per cent) and chemicals. Ivanovo region is very important producer of cotton manufactures, about one third of the total production for the USSR.

15. IRKUTSK. 767,900 sq. km. 1,979,000 inhabitants (62 per cent urban). Its main industries are timber and wood-processing which employs about 40.4 per cent of the total industrial labour force. It is based on its rich forests which cover about 75 per cent of area. Other important industries are metalworking and engineering (about 25 per cent), mining (11.6 per cent extracting coal, gold, iron ore, mica, first in the USSR and salt), food processing (8.1 per cent producing meat, fat, fish, flour, etc.), clothing (4.1 per cent), building materials (4.5 per cent), electricity generation (2.6

per cent). River Angara, the biggest potential power resource in the USSR.

16. KABARDINO-BALKARSK. (Capital: Nalchik). 12,519 sq. km. 420,000 inhabitants (38 per cent urban). Its most important industries are food processing employing about 20 per cent of total industrial labour force (animal and vegetable oil, meat, cheese, wine, tinned food). Other important industries are timber and wood processing (18 per cent), engineering and metalworking (16 per cent), building materials 9 per cent (bricks, limestone, cement), textiles and some coal-mining. It has very rich water resources and produces about 150 mill. Kwh. annually.

17. KALININGRAD. (formerly Konigsberg) 15,100 sq. km. 610,000 inhabitants (64 per cent urban). Its main industries are engineering and metalworking (producing transport equipment, fishing equipment, paper industry equipment, etc.), wood processing electricity generation, gas and coke, shipbuilding and ship repairs, food processing (beer, meat, flour, fish processing) and fishing.

18. KALININ. 83,105 sq. km. 1,802,000 inhabitants (44 per cent urban). Its main industries are textiles employing about 21.5 per cent of the total industrial labour force (cotton and linen fabrics, knitwear and rayon), engineering 13.6 per cent (wagons, agricultural machinery, mining equipment, textile and building machinery), food processing 6.4 per cent (fat, dairy products, flour-milling, alcohol, meat), timber and wood processing 11.6 per cent (saw mill products, paper, furniture, pre-fab houses), glass and porcelain (7 per cent), clothing (7 per cent), chemicals 5 per cent (synthetic fibre and rubber), mining (peat), metalworking (6.6. per cent), electricity generation and building materials.

19. KALUGA. 29,800 sq. km. 936,000 inhabitants (37 per cent urban). Mainly agricultural. Its main industries are timber and wood processing, engineering and metalworking (cranes, transport equipment, various machinery), food processing (meat, beer, vodka, alcohol), building materials, glass and porcelain, textiles (woollen fabrics, clothing), and mining (peat, brown coal).

20. KAMCHATKA. (Capital: Petropavlovsk - Kamchatskii). 472,200 sq. km. 220,000 inhabitants (64 per cent urban). The most important industries are fishing and fish processing (80 per

E

cent of total gross industrial output). There are other industries mainly servicing its fishing industry (ship repairing) and also timber and wood processing industries (5 per cent). Production of furs is also important.

21. KARELIA. (Capital: Petrozavodsk). 172,400 sq. km. 649,000 inhabitants (63 per cent urban). Its best developed industries are timber (30 per cent of gross industrial output), wood processing (about 15 per cent), paper and cellulose (13 per cent producing plywood, pre-fabricated houses, furniture etc.). The above account for about 10 per cent of the USSR production of these industries. Other industries are metalworking (12.5 per cent), electricity generation (1.4 per cent), clothing and knitwear (10 per cent), food processing 9.8 per cent (fish) and non-metallic minerals (6.2 per cent).

22. KEMEROVO. 95,500 sq. km. 2,788,000 inhabitants (77 per cent urban). Its most important industry is coal mining (hard coal—the richest coal basin in the USSR—the Kuzbass).   Other industries are mining of iron-ore, copper-ore, gold, zinc and bauxite, ferrous and non-ferrous metallurgy (pig-iron, rolling mill products, aluminium), chemicals (processing coal), engineering (coal-mining machinery and equipment), food processing (flour mills, alcohol, beer), light industries (clothing, tobacco, etc.) and electricity generation.

23. KIROV. 122,400 sq. km. 1,919,000 inhabitants (37 per cent urban). About 53 per cent of the Kirov surface area is covered by forests, therefore its most important industries are timber and wood-processing.   Other important industries are mining (iron-ore, phosphorite, copper ore and peat), engineering and metalworking and electricity generation (peat). Other industries are: leather, footwear, furs, textiles, etc.

24. KOMI. Capital: Syktyvkar. 411,500 sq. km. 804,000 inhabitants (59 per cent urban). The most important industries are coal mining (employing about 30 per cent of the total industrial labour force) exploiting the important Pechora coal basin, timber and wood processing (47.2 per cent), oil extracting and refining and gas industry (3.9 per cent), metalworking (5.9 per cent) and electricity generation.

25. KOSTROMA. 59,400 sq. km. 919,000 inhabitants (39 per cent urban). Agricultural area. Its main industries are textiles

(28 per cent of gross industrial output, mainly linen), timber and wood processing (30 per cent), food processing (18 per cent produces flour, beer, alcohol, meat), metalworking (8 per cent). Other industries are electricity generation, chemicals (processing wood) and building materials (bricks, glass).

26.   KRASNODAR.   83,700 sq. km. 3,766,000 inhabitants (39 per cent urban). Rich agricultural area. The most important industries are engineering (in 1950, 32 per cent of gross industrial output: equipment for oil industry, machine tools, printing machinery, tractors and ship repairs), and extracting and refining of oil. Other important industries are food processing (flour mills, fat, beer, sugar, wine, tobacco and tea), building materials (cement), wood processing and textiles. Fishing is also important.

27.   KRASNOYARSK.   2,573,000 sq. km.   2,786,000 inhabitants (48 per cent urban). The most important industries are timber and wood processing, engineering (heavy machinery, ship building, combines, equipment for mining and timber industries), mining (coal, iron-ore, gold, mica, salt, etc.), food processing (flour mills, tinned food, fat, alcohol, beer, fish processing, tobacco), building materials (bricks, pipes, cement), light industries (cotton fabrics, leather, footwear, etc.), electricity generation (thermal and hydro).

28.   KUIBYSHEV.   53,800 sq. km.   2,257,000 inhabitants (62 per cent urban). It is very important for its engineering, metalworking, oil-extracting and gas industries. In 1950 these industries accounted for about 84 per cent of the total gross industrial output. Electricity generating industry is well developed especially hydro (Kuibyshev hydro-electric plant—claimed to be the biggest in the world). Other industries are building materials, chemical and light industries (flour mills, sugar, wine, beer, vegetable oil, knitwear and footwear).

29.   KURGAN.   71,000 sq. km.   1,002,000 inhabitants (33 per cent urban). Still relatively undeveloped. Its important industries are engineering and metalworking (agricultural machines) food processing (tinned meat, dairy-products, flour mills, fat, etc.), building materials (bricks, tile, asphalt), light industries (footwear, clothing, knitwear) and electricity generation (thermal).

30.   KURSK.   29,800 sq. km. 1,481,000 inhabitants (20 per cent urban). Its main industries are engineering and metalworking

(about 39 per cent of the gross industrial output), food processing (about 35 per cent producing sugar, bread, vegetable oil), chemicals 12.7 per cent (phosphates), building materials (chalk, bricks), and light industries (textiles, wood processing, clothing, leather footwear). Iron ore mining is developing.

31. LENINGRAD. 197,700 sq. km. 6,225,000 inhabitants (72 per cent urban). Comprises the Leningrad, Novgorod and Pskov provinces. Its economic pattern is determined by Leningrad the second biggest industrial centre in the USSR Its main industries are engineering and metalworking, food processing (meat, wine, dairy products), textiles (especially important for linen), wood processing (paper), electricity generation (using rich deposits of peat mostly cut in Novgorod province), chemicals (synthetic rubber), building materials and fishing.

32. LIPETSK. 24,100 sq. km. 1,144,000 inhabitants (30 per cent urban). Its main industries are metallurgy (based on the rich deposits of iron-ore, produces pig-iron, pipes, etc.), engineering (tractors, machine tools, equipment), food processing (sugar, beer, alcohol) and building materials (cement, limestone).

33. MAGADAN. 1,224,500 sq. km. 235,000 inhabitants (81 per cent urban). Its main industries are fishing and fish processing, mining (gold, hard coal), some engineering and metalworking (mainly equipment for mining industry), building materials (glass) and electricity generation.

34. MARY (Capital: Yoshkar-Ola). 23,200 sq. km. 647,000 inhabitants (28 per cent urban). Largely agricultural. Its main industries are food processing (accounts for about 18.2 per cent of the total gross industrial output) and above all timber and wood processing about 54.4 per cent (paper, cellulose and is one of the biggest producers in the USSR), engineering and metalworking (17.1 per cent), building materials (glass) and peat mining.

35. MORDVA. (Capital: Saransk). 26,100 sq. km. 999,000 inhabitants (18 per cent urban). Poorly developed. Its most important industries are timber and wood processing (employing about 27.5 per cent of the total industrial labour force), food processing about 15.3 per cent (tinned food, meat, dairy products, fat, alcohol), engineering and metalworking 22.6 per cent (electrical appliances),

light industries 20 per cent (clothing, fabrics), building materials and fuel (peat).

36. MOSCOW (Town) 5,068,000 inhabitants. Gross industrial output is about 13 per cent of the USSR total.   Its most important industries are engineering and metalworking (employing about 47.4 per cent of the total industrial labour force and producing various electrical machinery, automobiles, instruments, watches, etc.) light 23.1 per cent (cotton fabrics, silk and woollen products, knitwear, leather footwear), food processing 6.3 per cent (meat, flour, vegetable oil, beer), chemicals 4.1 per cent (synthetic rubber, pharmaceuticals), printing (3.9 per cent), wood processing (2.9 per cent), building materials and electricity generation.

37. MOSCOW (Province). 46,900 sq. km. 5,870,000 inhabitants (56 per cent urban). Its most important industries are engineering and metalworking (employing about 29.8 per cent of the total industrial labour force, and producing steam and electric locomotives various heavy machinery, sawing-machines, television sets, etc.), textiles 30.2 per cent (cotton fabrics, silk and woollen fabrics, knitwear), chemicals 5.7 per cent (sulphuric acid, synthetic fibre and rubber, phosphate), food processing 2.2 per cent (fish, meat, confectionery). Other industries are building materials (6.6 per cent), electricity generation, mining (peat), metallurgy and other minor industries.

38. MURMANSK 144,900 sq. km. 567,000 inhabitants (92 per cent urban). The most important industries are fishing and fish processing (in 1952, 55 per cent of the total gross industrial output), mining (nickel, and other non-ferrous ores and iron ore, employing about 10 per cent of the total industrial labour force), timber and wood processing (17.1 per cent), metalworking (10.9 per cent). Other industries are electricity generation, clothing and building materials.

39. NOVOSIBIRSK.   178,200 sq. km.   2,299,000 inhabitants (55 per cent urban). A most important centre of engineering (tractors and agricultural machinery) and metallurgy (pig iron, non-ferrous metals, rolled steel). Also building materials (pipes, tiles, cement), timber and wood processing (sawn wood products), light (footwear, leather, knitwear, clothing, radio sets, furniture) and food processing (fats, flour, fish processing, meat, tinned food). Electricity generating

industry uses either imported coal from Kuzbas or water resources of the river Ob.

40. OMSK. 139,600 sq. km. 1,646,000 inhabitants (43 per cent urban). Its main industries are engineering (employing about 49 per cent of the total industrial labour force and producing about 35 per cent of the total gross industrial output) and metalworking. Other industries are textiles (5.2 per cent), clothing (6.2 per cent), wood processing (4.9 per cent), building materials (5 per cent), food processing (4.2 per cent) and electricity generation.

41. ORENBURG (formerly Chkalov). 123,800 sq. km. 1,831,000 inhabitants (45 per cent urban). Its main industries are engineering and metalworking (about 21.6 per cent of the total gross industrial output—metallurgical equipment, machine tools, transport equipment, etc.), food processing 18 per cent (meat, fish, animal and vegetable oil, tinned food, salt, flour), light industries 16.3 per cent (footwear knitwear, silk, clothing), ferrous and non-ferrous metallurgy 15.8 per cent (nickel, copper, pig iron), fuel 14.3 per cent (hard coal, gas and oil refining), electricity generation (3.6 per cent), timber and wood processing (3.5 per cent).

42. OREL. 24,700 sq. km. 926,000 inhabitants (24 per cent urban). Mainly agricultural. Its most important industries are engineering and metalworking (employing about 44 per cent of the total industrial labour force, and producing machine tools, agricultural machinery, clocks and watches, aluminium products), food processing 13.5 per cent (fat, vegetables, meat, flour, cheese, confectionery, alcohol, vodka, beer), building materials (9.4 per cent), clothing and knitwear (9 per cent) and wood processing (5.1 per cent). Other industries are electricity generation, footwear, etc.

43. PENZA. 43,300 sq. km. 1,510,000 inhabitants (33 per cent urban). Agricultural area. Its main industries are engineering and metalworking (employing about 49.4 per cent of the total industrial labour force and producing mining equipment, textile machinery clocks and watches, bicycles, tractors, agricultural machinery, lorries), food processing 8.6 per cent (sugar, meat, animal fat, cheese, confectionery, flour, vodka, beer), timber and wood processing 12.2 per cent (timber haulage, sawmill products, pre-fabricated houses, furniture, plywood) and textiles (8.1 per cent).

44. PERM (formerly Molotov). 162,600 sq. km. 2,998,000 inhabitants (59 per cent urban). Its most important industries are engineering and metalworking (account for about 18.4 per cent of total gross industrial output, producing excavators, electric engines, mining and oil industry equipment, tractors, etc.), timber and wood processing (14.6 per cent), metallurgy (10.3 per cent), food processing (11.8 per cent), chemicals (8.5 per cent), paper (8 per cent), coal mining (6.6. per cent Kizelov coal basin). Other industries are clothing, non-ferrous metallurgy, leather footwear, oil extracting and refining and electricity generation.

45. PRIMORSKII (Maritime province). Capital: Vladivostok. 165,900 sq. km. 1,379,000 inhabitants (67 per cent urban). Its main industries are fishing (accounts for about 33 per cent of the gross industrial output), food processing (55 per cent mainly fish-processing industry), mining 9.5 per cent (coal) and timber and wood processing industry. Some shipbuilding. Fish processing and other industries are concentrated in Vladivostok.

46. ROSTOV. 100,800 sq. km. 3,314,000 inhabitants (57 per cent urban). Its most important industries are engineering and metalworking (accounts for about 55 per cent of the total gross industrial output and produces pig-iron, rolling mill products, agricultural machinery, forging and stamping machines, mining equipment etc.), food processing 22.7 per cent (flour, tinned food), leather and footwear (10.5 per cent), clothing (7.8 per cent). Other industries are wood processing, building materials, coal mining and electricity generation.

47. RYAZAN. 39,700 sq. km. 1,441,000 inhabitants (30 per cent urban). Agricultural area. Its main industries are food processing (accounts for about 30.6 per cent of the total gross industrial output and produces flour, sugar, meat, fish, animal fat), light 29 per cent (clothings, knitwear, cotton fabrics, jute, footwear, leather and furs) and engineering and metalworking (17.5 per cent).

48. SARATOV. 100,200 sq. km. 2,167,000 inhabitants (54 per cent urban). The most important industries are engineering and metalworking (bearings, machine tools, cranes, buses, machinery for the oil refining industry, etc.), food-processing (flour, fats, meat), and electricity generation (on the river Volga). Other industries

are light (clothing, knitwear, cotton fabrics), oil extracting and refining, gas, building materials, chemicals (alcohol, rubber).

49. SAKHALIN. Capital: Yuzhno-Sakhalinsk. 87,000 sq. km. 651,000 inhabitants (75 per cent urban). Its main industries are food processing (about 36.6 per cent of the total gross industrial output for Sakhalin), fishing (15 per cent including also whale fishing), wood processing (4.1 per cent), paper (15.4 per cent), timber (7.6 per cent), coal mining (17.8 per cent), oil extracting (4.1 per cent).

50. SVERDLOVSK. 192,800 sq. km. 4,048,000 inhabitants (76 per cent urban). Sverdlovsk is one of the most important industrial regions in the USSR. Its most important industries are ferrous and non-ferrous metallurgy (37.2 per cent of the gross industrial output producing pig-iron, steel, copper, aluminium), engineering and metalworking (about 20.5 per cent), and wood processing. Other industries are food processing (9.0 per cent), mining 4.2 per cent (iron ore, hard coal), fuel, light, building materials, electricity generation and printing.

51. SEVERO-OSETINSKI (North Ossetia). Capital: Ordzhonikidze. 8,000 sq. km. 449,000 inhabitants (53 per cent urban). Its industrial pattern is determined by the rich local resources of raw-materials, timber and water power. Its main industries are food processing (34 per cent of the total gross industrial output) non-ferrous metals (25.7 per cent), clothing (10.9 per cent), metalworking (7.2 per cent), wood processing (5.1 per cent), and oil extracting (2.3 per cent).

52. SMOLENSK. 49,900 sq. km. 1,140,000 inhabitants (32 per cent urban). Largely agricultural. Its main industries are food processing. (38 per cent of the total industrial output and produces dairy products, fats, meat, fish), light industries—29.6 per cent (textiles 13.9 per cent, clothing 13.3 per cent, leather, furs and footwear 2.4 per cent), engineering and metalworking (10.2 per cent), timber and wood processing (10.6 per cent). Other industries are electricity generation, fuel (peat, hard coal), building materials, glass and printing.

53. STAVROPOL. 156,400 sq. km. 2,069,000 inhabitants (29 per cent urban). Rich agricultural area. Its most important industries are food processing (about 39.3 per cent of the total gross industrial

output producing flour, vegetable oil, tinned meat), textiles 25.3 per cent (of which wool 23.8 per cent one of the biggest producers in the USSR), metalworking 10.4 per cent (agricultural machinery and transport equipment), clothing (7.8 per cent), timber (5.3 per cent). Other industries are chemicals, building materials, leather footwear, and mining (coal, oil, salt, etc.). Stavropol is very important for the production of natural gas, it is connected by gas-pipes with many industrial centres and it also supplies Moscow.

54. STALINGRAD. 114,100 sq. km. 1,849,000 inhabitants (54 per cent urban). Its most important industries are engineering and metalworking (about 35 per cent of the total gross industrial output produces tractors, ships, equipment for oil industry), ferrous metallurgy 13.5 per cent (steel, rolling mill products), and food processing 22.5 per cent (vegetable oil, tinned food, meat, fish). Other industries are light 7.8 per cent (clothing, footwear, knitwear, leather), building materials, chemicals, wood-processing, oil extracting and refining.

55. TAMBOV. 34,300 sq. km. 1,547,000 inhabitants (26 per cent urban). Little developed farming area. Its most important industries are food-processing (about 36 per cent of the total gross industrial output) engineering and metalworking 21.4 per cent (various equipment, washing machines, etc.), textiles 12.6 per cent (of which wool 10.6 per cent), and chemicals 12.8 per cent (synthetic rubber).

56. TATAR. (Capital: Kazan). 68,000 sq. km. 2,847,000 inhabitants (42 per cent urban). It is of great importance for oil and natural gas. There are also textiles (cotton and linen fabrics), light (leather, footwear, furs), food processing (meat, butter, fish), engineering and metalworking (road building equipment, aircraft, typewriters, clocks and watches, agricultural machinery), and building materials.

57. TOMSK. 316,900 sq. km. 750,000 inhabitants (47 per cent urban). Over 54 per cent of the surface area is covered by forests. Its most important industries are timber and wood processing (about 28 per cent of the total gross industrial output) metalworking 26 per cent (equipment for coal industry), food processing 20.2 per cent (fish processing, meat, fat, flour, tinned food), mining (iron-ore). Other industries are clothing 6.7 per cent (knitwear), chemicals and building materials.

58. TULA. 25,700 sq. km. 1,912,000 inhabitants (61 per cent urban). Its main industries are engineering and metalworking (accounts for about 28.1 per cent of the total gross industrial output and produces household utensils, machine tools, mining and agricultural machinery), coal-mining (13.8 per cent), chemicals 10.3 per cent (synthetic rubber), power generation (7.2 per cent) and metallurgy 6.4 per cent (pipes, pig iron). Other industries are food processing (18.5 per cent), building materials.

59. TYUMEN. 1,435,300 sq. km. 1,094,000 inhabitants (32 per cent urban). Its main industries are food processing (35 per cent of total gross industrial output and produces fish 5.1 per cent, tinned food 11.2 per cent, fats), timber and wood processing 26.2 per cent (sawmill products, plywood, furniture), engineering and metalworking 20.8 per cent (shipbuilding, building equipment, tractors).

60. UDMURT Capital: Izhevsk. 42,100 sq. km. 1,333,000 inhabitants (44 per cent urban). Its most important industries are engineering and metalworking (42.7 per cent of the total gross industrial output and produces machine tools, steam locomotives, statutory engines, motor-cycles, radio sets), metallurgy (14.3 per cent) and timber and wood-processing 10.2 per cent (sawmill products). Other industries are food processing, building materials, clothing and textiles and electricity generation (peat).

61. ULYANOVSK. 37,200 sq. km. 1,118,000 inhabitants (36 per cent urban). Its main industries are engineering (32.9 per cent of the total gross industrial output and produces machine-tools, automobiles, cranes, agricultural machinery), textiles (19.2 per cent), food-processing 16.7 per cent (flour, fats, meat, fish, alcohol and beer) and clothing (11.9 per cent). Other industries are wood processing (paper, pre-fab. houses, sawmill products), chemicals, building materials.

62. KHABAROVSK. 824,500 sq. km. 1,143,000 inhabitants (74 per cent urban). Its main industries are food processing and fishing on the Okhotsk sea (employs about 25 per cent of the total industrial labour force). Other industries are engineering and metalworking 32.8 per cent (shipbuilding and building of fishing boats, machinery and equipment for mining), timber and wood processing (24.8 per cent), ferrous and non-ferrous metallurgy (6.4 per cent), light 6.9 per cent (cotton fabrics, footwear, knitwear).

63. CHELYABINSK.   88,300 sq. km.   2,982,000 inhabitants (76 per cent urban). Its most important industry is metallurgy (iron-ore from Ural) which is one of the biggest in the world, including the Magnitogorsk combine. It accounts for about 32 per cent of the total gross industrial output. Other important industries are engineering and metalworking (24 per cent), non-ferrous metallurgy (copper, nickel, zinc), food processing (10.8 per cent), building materials, timber and wood-processing, clothing (3.2 per cent), chemicals 3.3 per cent (fertilisers), electricity generation and coal mining (3.3 per cent) 'Chelyabinsk Basin'.

64. CHECHENO-INGUSH.   Capital: Groznyi.   19,300 sq. km. 711,000 inhabitants (41 per cent urban). The most important industries are oil and gas; employing about 26 per cent of the total industrial labour force. Engineering and metalworking industries (mostly oil equipment) employ about 21 per cent.   Groznyi is very important centre for oil industry. Also timber and wood processing.

65. CHITA.   43,5000 sq. km.   1,039,000 inhabitants (55 per cent urban). The most important industry is mining (tin, gold, iron ore, coal, lead), non-ferrous and ferrous metallurgy, food processing (meat, flour, macaroni), and wood processing.

66. CHUVASH.   Capital: Cheboksary.   18,300 sq. km.   1,098,000 inhabitants (24 per cent urban).   Largely agricultural.   Its main industries are engineering and metalworking (15 per cent of the total gross industrial output producing steam locomotives, television sets, washing machines, etc.), food processing 22 per cent (vodka, beer, meat, flour, alcohol, confectionery), wood processing (16 per cent), chemicals (11 per cent) and textiles 12 per cent (cotton fabrics, clothing, stockings).   Other industries are building materials, fuel (peat) and electricity generation. Fishing on the Caspian Sea is also important.

67. YAKUTIA.   3,077,800 sq. km.   489,000 inhabitants (49 per cent urban). Arctic and remote.   Its most important industries are food processing (21.4 per cent of the total gross industrial output), metalworking (12.2 per cent mostly ship repairing), electricity generation (10.4 per cent), timber and wood processing (7.8 per cent) and coal mining (3.7 per cent). Very important industries are gold mining and diamonds (the biggest producer of diamonds in the USSR).

68. YAROSLAV. 37,200 sq. km. 1,395,000 inhabitants (58 per cent urban). The most important industries are chemicals (synthetic rubber, asbestos, oil refining), engineering (automobiles, electrical machines, printing machinery) and textiles (cotton fabrics, linen). Other industries are food processing (dairy products, tinned food) and building materials (bricks, porcelain).

B. THE UKRAINIAN SOVIET SOCIALIST REPUBLIC

The Ukraine, 601,000 sq. km. 41,893,000 inhabitants, is divided into eleven Economic Administrative Regions or 'Sovnarkhozy': Ukrainian gross industrial output accounts for about 20.2 per cent of the total for the USSR.

1. STALINO. 26,500 sq. km. 4,265,000 inhabitants (86 per cent urban). The region with the greatest share of the gross industrial output in the Ukraine (20 per cent). The most important industries are coal mining (55 per cent of gross industrial output), engineering and metal working (11.5 per cent), building materials (36 per cent), and chemicals (17 per cent). The Stalino region is an important producer of fire resistant building materials for metallurgy (fire-clay, magnesium, bricks, etc.).

2. LUGANSK (formerly Voroshilovgrad) 32,000 sq. km. 2,457,000 inhabitants (79 per cent urban). Its industry is very similar to that of Stalino region but on a smaller scale (8 per cent of Ukrainian gross industrial output). The main industries are fuel (47 per cent of gross industrial output) machinery, diesel engines (16.6 per cent) and chemicals (7 per cent). The Lugansk region produces 40 per cent of the Ukrainian coal, 18 per cent of chemical products and 6.5 per cent of machinery.

3. DNEPROPETROVSK. 32,000 sq. km. 2,708,000 inhabitants (70 per cent urban). An important producer of iron ore (Krivoi Rog) and manganese, supplying many parts of the USSR. The machinery and metalworking industry is one of the biggest in the Ukraine (12.6 per cent of Ukrainian production). This region is closely connected with the Donbas region to which it exports iron and manganese ore and from which it imports coal, fire-clay, etc. It produces 11 per cent of the gross industrial output for the Ukraine.

4. ZAPOROZHE. 27,000 sq. km. 1,466,000 inhabitants (57 per cent urban). The industry of the region differs from that of the above

three regions. Although close to the oldest coal and metal producing region of the USSR it does not possess any iron ore and coal. The most important industries are metallurgy (36.4 per cent of gross industrial output), machinery and metalworking (23.4 per cent), fuel (coke), food processing (10.2 per cent), light industry (10 per cent) and non-ferrous metals all using electricity from the Dnieper dam. It produces about 6 per cent of the total Ukrainian gross industrial output.

5. KHARKOV. 84,700 sq. km. 5,659,000 inhabitants (45 per cent urban). It comprises Kharkov, Poltava and the Sumi provinces. The Kharkov region is one of the most important centres for the machine-building industry in the USSR, producing complicated machinery, machine tools, electro-technical equipment. Besides the most important machine building and metalworking industries (26 per cent of gross industrial output) there are some other well developed industries: food processing (19 per cent) and light industry (23 per cent). The important industrial centres are Kharkov (one of the biggest in the USSR), Sumi, Poltava, Konotop, Romni and others. It accounts for 15.4 per cent of the gross industrial output of the Ukraine.

6. KIEV. 135,100 sq. km. 8,699,000 inhabitants (35 per cent urban). It includes the Kiev, Zhitomir, Chernigov, Cherkassi and Kirovograd provinces. The most important industries are machinery and metalworking (accounting for 14 per cent of the total Ukrainian output of machinery and metals), food processing industry (21 per cent of gross industrial output), timber and wood processing (20 per cent), chemicals (20 per cent) and building materials. Coal mining has been only recently developed with an annual production of 10 million tons. The region accounts for 15.2 per cent of the total gross industrial output of the Ukraine.

7. VINNITSA. 47,700 sq. km. 3,750,000 inhabitants (18 per cent urban). Comprises the Vinnitsa and Khmelnitskii provinces. Its small industry is based on the local agricultural production of sugar-beet, vegetables, fruits and live-stock and dairy products. The food processing industry (sugar, alcohol, tinned food, etc.) is the most important one (62 per cent of gross industrial output). Other industries are machinery and metalworking (8 per cent) and light

industry (15 per cent). The gross industrial output of Vinnitsa region represents only 3.7 per cent of the Ukrainian one.

8. ODESSA. 33,100 sq. km. 2,028,000 inhabitants (47 per cent urban). Its economic pattern is determined by the town of Odessa, a big port on the Black Sea. The most important industries are food processing, 36 per cent of gross industrial output (fish, tinned food, wine, etc.), light industry (24 per cent), machinery and metalworking (23 per cent) and chemicals. This region is locally important in the Ukraine for the production of machine tools for metal and wood working, stamping machines, railway and auto cranes, agricultural machines etc. The region produces 5.6 per cent of the Ukrainian gross industrial output.

9. KHERSON. 77,600 sq. km. 3,044,000 inhabitants (49 per cent urban). It comprises Kherson, Nikolaev and Crimean provinces. The machinery and metalworking industries account for the biggest part of the region's gross industrial output (36 per cent), mainly ships and road-building equipment. The food processing industry (30 per cent) is also very important, based on the local supply of food-stuffs, producing mainly tinned food and wine (Crimea). A new textile mill has been built in Kherson city. The region accounts for 5.9 per cent of total Ukrainian gross industrial output.

10. LVOV. 66,300 sq. km. 4,173,000 inhabitants (27 per cent urban). It comprises the Lvov, Volhynia, Rovno and Ternopol provinces. The Lvov region is mostly agricultural with only recently developed industries of which the food processing industry (37 per cent of the total industrial output) is the most important, based on the local agricultural production of sugar-beet, potatoes and live-stock and dairy produce. There is also some light industry (22 per cent), machinery and metalworking (17 per cent) and timber and wood manufacture industry based on the vast resources of wood. Its share in the Ukrainian industrial output is only 4.6 per cent.

11. STANISLAVOV. 44,300 sq. km. 3,644,000 inhabitants (26 per cent urban). It comprises the Stanislavov, Chernovtsi and Zakarpatski provinces. It is mostly agricultural. The existing industry is based on local resources, notably timber and wood processing (26 per cent of the Ukrainian wood production), oil, gas, and salt extracting, chemicals, textiles and building materials

(cement). Accounts for 4.8 per cent of the Ukrainian gross industrial output.

C. KAZAKH SOVIET SOCIALIST REPUBLIC   (Kazakhstan) 2,756,000 sq. km. 9,301,000 inhabitants (44 per cent urban), is divided into nine Economic Administrative Regions of 'Sovnark-hozy'. Its gross industrial output accounts for about 3.4 per cent of the total for the USSR. Its northern regions have been the scene of the vast 'virgin lands campaign', expanding area sown to grain several-fold since 1954.

1. ALMA-ATA 374,000 sq. km. 1,940,000 inhabitants (43 per cent urban). Comprises the Alma-Ata, Dzhambul and Taldy-Kurgan provinces. It has very rich deposits of phosphates, metal ores, gypsum, limestone, marble and others. Industries are machine building, metalworking, mining and chemicals. Light and food processing industries are also well developed because irrigation makes possible the growth of foodstuffs and industrial crops (tobacco, sugar-beet), producing sugar, wine, tinned food, tobacco, leather, footwear and others. Accounts for about 18.3 per cent of the Kazakhstan industrial output.

2. SEMIPALATINSK. 168,000 sq. km. 487,000 inhabitants (47 per cent urban). Has mostly light and food processing industries producing leather, sheep-skins leather footwear, raw wool, tinned meat and others, production of which is based upon the local supply of agricultural products. Its future development plans are mostly concerned with the expansion of light and food processing industries. The gross industrial output of the region represents about 9.4 per cent of the total for Kazakhstan.

3. EAST-KAZAKHSTAN. Capital : Ust-Kamenogorsk. 97,000 sq. km. 732,000 inhabitants (54 per cent urban). Its non-ferrous metals industry is based on rich deposits of lead, zinc, copper and precious metals. Mining of hard coal and shale-oil is well developed and these together with the electricity generation (based on rich resources of water power), supply power to the non-ferrous and chemical industries. Gross industrial output accounts for about 12.7 per cent of the total for Kazakhstan.

4. KARAGANDA. 689,000 sq. km. 2,146,000 inhabitants (56 per cent urban). Comprises the Karaganda, Akmolinsk and Pavlodar

provinces. It produces more than a quarter (29.3 per cent) of Kazakhstan's gross industrial output. The most important industries are coal-mining and metallurgy. The Karaganda coal basin is one of the three biggest of the USSR. Karaganda is also the most important producer of copper in the USSR. Other industries are machine building, chemicals, ferrous and non-ferrous rolling mill products and building materials (cement).

5. NORTH-KAZAKHSTAN. Capital : Petropavlovsk. 120,000 sq. km. 945,000 inhabitants (29 per cent urban). Comprises the North-Kazakhstan and Kokchetav provinces. Food processing and light industries are well developed and abundantly supplied by the local livestock products and crops grown on the 13 million acres of arable land. Besides these there are some engineering and power generation. Gross industrial output accounts for about 6.5 per cent of the total for Kazakhstan.

6. KUSTANAI. 196,000 sq. km. 705,000 inhabitants (27 per cent urban). Industry still small. It is a predominantly agricultural region though large iron ore deposits are being developed. Its share of the gross industrial output of Kazakhstan is small (about 2.7 per cent).

7. AKTYUBINSK. 452,000 sq. km. 787,000 inhabitants (37 per cent urban). Comprises the Aktyubinsk and West-Kazakhstan provinces. The existing industries are metallurgy, machine building, chemicals, light and food processing industries. There are rich deposits of chrome, nickel, copper, iron-ore, cobalt, oil, asbestos and others, exploitation of which is being expanded. Gross industrial output accounts for about 5.1 per cent of the total for Kazakhstan.

8. GURYEV. 278,000 sq. km. 288,000 inhabitants (56 per cent urban). Its main industries are oil extracting and fishing which account for more than three-quarters of the total industrial output of Guryev. It has very rich deposits of oil and other minerals (salt coal, phosphates, etc.) and good fishing places all along the Ural and on the Caspian Sea. Gross industrial output accounts for about 3.5 per cent of the total for Kazakhstan.

9. SOUTH-KAZAKHSTAN. Capital: Chimkent. 382,000 sq. km. 1,253,000 inhabitants (39 per cent urban). Comprises the South-Kazakhstan and Kzyl-Orda provinces. Its gross industrial

output accounts for about 12.5 per cent of the total for Kazakhstan. The main industries are non-ferrous metals, mining (especially coal), machine building and the production of building materials. Light and food processing industries (cotton fabrics, paper, clothing, footwear, fish, tinned fruit, etc.) which are based on the local supply of relevant materials.

D.   UZBEKISTAN.   Capital: Tashkent. 409,400 sq. km. 8,113,000 inhabitants (34 per cent urban). It is divided into five Administrative Economic Regions—'Sovnarkhozy'. The gross industrial output for Uzbekistan accounts for about 1.7 per cent of the total for the USSR.   It is of great importance in cotton-growing on irrigated land.

1.   TASHKENT. 20,500 sq. km. 2,263,000 inhabitants (58 per cent urban). Comprises the province and town Tashkent. Its gross industrial output accounts for about 40 per cent of the total for Uzbekistan. Its main industries are electricity generation (about 90 per cent of Uzbek production). Textiles (knitwear, cotton textiles), coal mining, ferrous and non-ferrous metallurgy (copper), engineering and metalworking (agricultural, mining, textile and chemical industries equipment and machinery, transport equipment and others), chemicals (electro-chemical combine—one of the biggest in the USSR), building materials (cement, bricks, limestone) and food processing industry (fats, flour mills, tinned food, etc.).

2.   FERGANA. 19,300 sq. km. 2,300,000 inhabitants (27 per cent urban). Comprises the Andizhan, Namangan and Fergana provinces. Fergana is the most important producer of oil for Uzbekistan and also of building materials (cement). Centre of cotton-growing and processing.   Also other textiles (silk). The gross industrial output of the region accounts for about 28.6 per cent of the total for Uzbekistan.

3.   KARA-KALPAK. Capital: Nukus. 160,600 sq. km. 890,000 inhabitants (22 per cent urban). Comprises the Kara-Kalpak and Khorezm provinces.   Its industrial pattern is determined by local production of raw cotton, silk, fish and livestock products; hence industries are cotton and silk processing, food processing (meat, animal fat, wine), and fishing on the Aral sea.   Gross industrial output accounts for about 7.7 per cent of the total for Uzbekistan.

F

4. SAMARKAND. 87,100 sq. km. 2,087,000 inhabitants (22 per cent urban). Comprises the Samarkand, Koshka-Darya and Surkhan-Darya provinces. The gross industrial output of the region accounts for about 16.1 per cent of the total for Uzbekistan. Existing industries are textiles (cotton and silk-processing, jute, knitwear), food processing (dairy products, tinned food, wine, alcohol, fat, meat, tea and tobacco) and some metalworking (parts for tractors and automobiles), non-ferrous metallurgy and oil extracting.

5. BUKHARA. 122,900 sq. km. 573,000 inhabitants (22 per cent urban). In January 1958 Bukhara province was detached from Samarkand Sovnarkhoz and established as a separate one. The gross industrial output of Bukhara accounts for about 7.8 per cent of the total for Uzbekistan. Large natural gas resources are being developed. Other industries are cotton processing, food processing (wine and meat combines), salt extracting, building materials and metalworking.

E. AZERBAIDZIAN. Capital: Baku. 86,600 sq. km. 3,700,000 inhabitants (48 per cent urban). Its gross industrial output accounts for about 3.1 per cent of the total for the USSR. Existing industries are oil extracting and refining (Baku—the second oil area in the USSR), gas, chemicals (alcohol, iodine), engineering (oil industry equipment and other machinery), mining (iron ore, cobalt), metalworking (pipes, aluminium), food processing and some textiles (based on an important local output of raw cotton).

F. ARMENIA. Capital: Erevan. 29,000 sq. km. 1,768,000 inhabitants (50 per cent urban). Its gross industrial output accounts for about 0.7 per cent of the total for the USSR. The existing industries are electricity generation (6.5 per cent of gross industrial output), non-ferrous metals, chemicals (17 per cent), engineering and metalworking (28 per cent), building materials and wood processing, food processing (17 per cent) and textiles (12 per cent). It has very rich deposits of metal and non-metal ores (copper, zinc, iron ore, precious metals, oil and quarrying materials).

G. BYELORUSSIA. Capital: Minsk. 207,600 sq. km. 8,600,000 inhabitants (31 per cent urban). Its gross industrial output accounts for about 1.6 per cent of the total for the USSR. Byelorussia is important for its wood processing industry and light industry processing agricultural products like linen, potato and dairy products. Other industries are power generation (using vast deposits of peat), fuel industry (peat), engineering and metalworking (25 per cent of gross industrial output producing various equipment, motor vehicles, tractors, various light machinery, motorcycles, cycles, etc.) food processing (over 20 per cent of gross industrial output). 28 per cent of the Byelorussian surface area is covered by forests and so forms a good base for the well developed timber and wood processing industries.

H. GEORGIA. Capital: Tbilisi (Tiflis). 69,700 sq. km. 4,049,000 inhabitants (42 per cent urban). Food processing and light industries are the best developed industries in Georgia both based on the local agricultural production of subtropical crops like tea, wine, fruits, tobacco, silk-cocoon and cotton. The food processing industry accounts for about 41.9 per cent (tea 11.9 per cent), and light industries for 22.2 per cent (silk 5.4 per cent) of gross industrial output. Other industries are machine building, metalworking and ferrous metallurgy (together 31 per cent). Gross industrial output accounts for about 1.8 per cent of the total for the USSR.

I. KIRGHIZ. Capital: Frunze. 198,500 sq. km. 2,063,000 inhabitants (34 per cent urban). Relatively undeveloped. The existing industries are mining (6.2 per cent of the gross industrial output), metalworking and machine building (18.2 per cent), food processing (26.8 per cent) and textiles (16.6 per cent). Last two industries are based on the local agricultural production of technical crops and foodstuffs. Other industries' products are coal, lead ore, dairy products, sugar, cotton, and silk manufactures. 60 per cent of the industrial production comes from the town of Frunze and Frunze province. Gross industrial output accounts for about 0.4 per cent of the total for the USSR.

J. LATVIA. Capital: Riga. 63,700 sq. km. 2,094,000 inhabitants (56 per cent urban). The existing industries are metalworking (employing about 25.1 per cent of Latvian labour force and producing electrical machines and appliances, wagons, ships, diesel engines, etc.), light (24.0 per cent of which most important is textile industry utilising imported silk, cotton and wool), timber and wood processing industries (12.1 per cent) and food processing industry (producing dairy products, meat, tinned fish and sugar). Gross industrial output accounts for about 0.8 per cent of the total for the USSR.

K. LITHUANIA. Capital: Vilnyus. 65,200 sq. km. 2,713,000 inhabitants (39 per cent urban). Its food processing industry accounts for more than one third of the Lithuanian gross industrial output and is very diversified. Produces meat, dairy products, sugar, etc. Other industries are light (32 per cent), engineering and metalworking (16.2 per cent), wood processing, coal mining (peat), electrotechnical, building materials, electricity generation (using peat and ample water resources) and fishing. Gross industrial output accounts for about 0.5 per cent of the total for the USSR.

L. MOLDAVIA. Capital: Kishinev. 33,700 sq. km. 2,880,000 inhabitants (22 per cent urban). Mostly agricultural. The most important industry is food processing which is based upon the intensive local agricultural production of wine, vegetables, fat, sugarbeet and it accounts for about 58.4 per cent of the total gross industrial output for Moldavia. Other industries were mostly developed after the second world war and they are light (leather, footwear, knitwear, clothing, furs), engineering, metalworking, building materials and electricity generation. Gross industrial output accounts for about 0.4 per cent of the total for the USSR.

M. TADZHIKISTAN. Capital: Stalinabad. 143,500 sq. km. 1,982,000 inhabitants (33 per cent urban). Industrially not well developed region although there are industries, e.g. food processing, light, building materials, metalworking, mining (lead, zinc, coal), textiles (Tadzhikistan is the second biggest producer of raw cotton in the USSR). The main products of the food processing industry are fats, wine, beer and alcohol. Gross industrial output accounts for about 0.3 per cent of the total for the USSR.

N. TURKMENISTAN. Capital: Ashkhabad. 488,000 sq. km. 1,520,000 inhabitants (46 per cent urban). Industrially not well developed region. Existing industries are textile industry, oil extracting and refining (13.4 per cent of the gross industrial output; Turkmenistan is the third biggest producer of crude oil in the USSR), food processing 21.8 per cent (meat, fat, salt), metalworking (5.7 per cent), chemicals 1.4 per cent (sulphur, iodine, bromine), electricity generation and building materials. Gross industrial output accounts for about 0.6 per cent of the total for the USSR.

O. ESTONIA. Capital: Tallin. 45,100 sq. km. 1,196,000 inhabitants (56 per cent urban). It has very intensive agriculture. It is the first in the USSR for the production and processing of shale-oil. Other industries are electricity generating, machine building, textiles, food processing, fishing, and wood processing. The gross industrial output of Estonia accounts for about 0.7 per cent of the total for the USSR.

Sources:
  Bolshaya Sovetskaia Entsiklopedia (Moscow 1950-1959).
  Ezhegodnik Sovetskoi Entsiklopedii for 1957 and 1958.
  RSFSR za 40 let—Statisticheskii Sbornik (1957).
  Promyshlenost SSSR, Statisticheskii Sbornik (1957).
  Kommunist Ukrainy No 6/1957.
  Planovoe Khozyaistvo No 9/1957.
  V. M. Kostennikov: Economic Regions of the USSR (Moscow 1958).
Narodnoe Khozyaistvo SSSR, 1958 godu (Moscow, 1959).
  Also statistical compendia for a total of 34 regions and provinces.

B. ORGANISATIONAL STRUCTURE OF THE SVERDLOVSK SOVNARKHOZ

SVERDLOVSK SOVNARKHOZ

TECHNICAL ECONOMIC COUNCIL

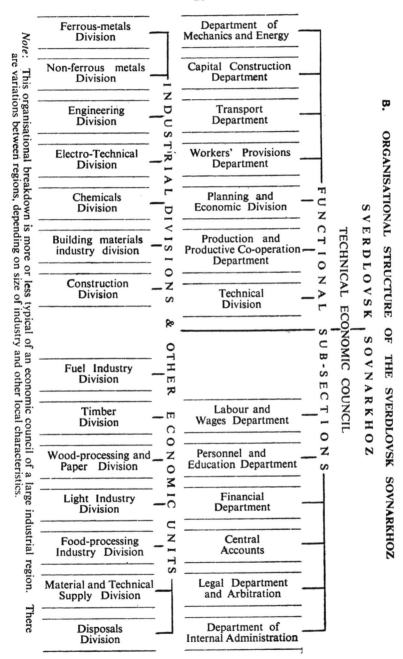

Note: This organisational breakdown is more or less typical of an economic council of a large industrial region. There are variations between regions, depending on size of industry and other local characteristics.

INDUSTRIAL DIVISIONS & OTHER ECONOMIC UNITS

- Ferrous-metals Division
- Non-ferrous metals Division
- Engineering Division
- Electro-Technical Division
- Chemicals Division
- Building materials industry division
- Construction Division
- Fuel Industry Division
- Timber Division
- Wood-processing and Paper Division
- Light Industry Division
- Food-processing Industry Division
- Material and Technical Supply Division
- Disposals Division

FUNCTIONAL SUB-SECTIONS

- Department of Mechanics and Energy
- Capital Construction Department
- Transport Department
- Workers' Provisions Department
- Planning and Economic Division
- Production and Productive Co-operation Department
- Technical Division
- Labour and Wages Department
- Personnel and Education Department
- Financial Department
- Central Accounts
- Legal Department and Arbitration
- Department of Internal Administration

Part III

External Trade Statistics

ACKNOWLEDGEMENT

Mr. D. Matko, of the Economic Research Division, London School of Economics, is thanked for valuable assistance in particular with the preparation of the tables.

89

A. Soviet External Trade

TABLE I, BY COUNTRY

(Millions of Roubles: 11·2 roubles=£1)

	1955		1956		1957		1958	
	IMPORTS	EXPORTS	IMPORTS	EXPORTS	IMPORTS	EXPORTS	IMPORTS	EXPORTS
BLOC COUNTRIES								
Albania	22	61	33	73	56	131	56	177
Bulgaria	486	510	579	434	792	690	812	802
Czechoslovakia	1,546	1,424	1,586	1,495	1,542	2,205	2,048	1,787
China	2,574	2,993	3,057	2,932	2,953	2,176	3,525	2,536
East Germany	2,026	1,915	2,505	2,285	3,057	3,448	3,264	3,199
Hungary	586	461	483	507	427	999	648	802
Mongolia	215	487	217	414	201	271	189	259
North Korea	163	177	205	215	250	240	188	232
North Vietnam	0	1	5	10	13	39	40	33
Poland	1,147	1,727	1,133	1,429	1,024	1,723	1,061	1,507
Rumania	839	1,071	941	848	760	1,003	934	1,006
TOTAL BLOC COUNTRIES	9,604	10,827	10,744	10,642	11,075	12,925	12,765	12,340
REST OF THE WORLD								
Austria	142	55	259	44	272	72	254	89
Belgium	61	97	128	117	123	113	65	92
Denmark	40	31	26	33	46	52	57	56
Finland	511	425	585	459	661	602	549	469
France	144	239	202	279	190	268	322	348
German Federal Republic	95	117	272	167	247	286	288	263
Iceland	40	41	50	40	55	46	44	50
Italy	65	70	104	136	182	117	141	154
Netherlands	138	131	40	167	82	181	71	228
Norway	60	70	86	78	72	84	65	69

Spain	—	—	—	—	—	—	20	22
Sweden	68	114	104	139	101	126	112	121
Yugoslavia	70	66	199	276	227	292	204	204
United Kingdom	284	677	298	593	448	705	292	582
Afghanistan	44	54	61	73	83	73	50	93
Burma	67	1	49	17	36	26	0	10
India	18	29	73	162	168	339	204	520
Indonesia	15	0	52	1	79	22	46	109
Iran	76	77	61	77	74	127	106	110
Japan	7	9	3	12	35	34	71	80
Malaya	87	0	336	1	195	2	472	0
Turkey	21	30	26	24	22	36	46	38
Yemen	0	0	0	1	3	5	2	5
Egypt and Syria	62	45	207	160	466	347	522	412
Ghana	46	0	33	0	76	0	11	0
Cameroons	—	—	—	—	0·3	—	26	0·1
Morocco	—	—	4	6	21	3	7	5
Union of South Africa	38	—	51	2	107	1	47	1
Canada	11	8	98	9	36	17	101	9
United States	2	95	19	109	41	64	19	41
Argentine	113	96	52	77	83	19	64	83
Cuba	143	—	59	—	188	—	62	—
Uruguay	40	1	49	11	73	1	99	22
New Zealand	16	—	34	—	32	—	22	—
TOTAL REST OF THE WORLD	2,638	3,047	3,709	3,804	4,676	4,601	4,634	4,850
TOTAL ALL COUNTRIES	12,242	13,874	14,453	14,446	15,751	17,526	17,399	17,190

A. Soviet External Trade

TABLE II, BY COMMODITY

EXPORTS

A. Commodity Groups

(Per cent of total)

	1938	1950	1955	1957	1958
Machinery and equipment	5·0	11·8	17·5	14·9	18·5
Fuel and raw materials	57·7	64·4	67·9	64·1	65·9
(Oil and oil products)	(7·8)	(2·4)	(6·7)	(9·1)	(10·0)
(Timber products)	(20·1)	(2·4)	(4·0)	(4·3)	(4·6)
Grain	21·3	12·1	8·3	12·9	8·3
Consumers' goods	16·0	11·7	6·3	8·1	7·3

B. Commodities

	1938	1950	1955	1957	1958
Passenger cars (thousands)	0·2	5·2	12·9	23·0	21·7
Lorries ,,	6·5	12·2	22·4	11·2	29·7
Coal	424	1121	4313	8772	9951
Crude oil	168	303	2916	5923	9093
Oil products	1221	778	5090	7757	9045
Iron ore	7	3227	8817	10773	11919
Manganese ore	446	277	851	806	833
Pig iron	6	397	1149	1278	1046
Rolling mill products (000 tons)	53	584	1511	1923	2162
Copper	—	n.a.	37	61	44
Aluminium	—	n.a.	42	85	115
Tin	—	n.a.	2	18	22
Lead	—	n.a.	26	55	62
Zinc	—	n.a.	36	72	66
Logs (thousand cu. metres)	1658	686	1637	2369	3024
Sawmill products ,, ,, ,,	3190	1042	2338	3457	3631
Raw cotton (thousand tons)	20	216	337	319	311
Grain ,, ,,	2054	2885	3683	7413	5100
Cotton fabrics (mill. metres)	157	80	137	178	166

92

A. Soviet External Trade

TABLE II, BY COMMODITY

IMPORTS

A. Commodity Groups
(Per cent of total)

			1938	1950	1955	1957	1958
Machinery and equipment	..		34·5	21·5	30·2	23·9	24·5
Fuel and raw materials	..	..	60·7	63·3	51·5	55·5	51·6
(Ores and concentrates)	..	..	(2·6)	(5·8)	(8·2)	(11·5)	(9·3)
(Metals)	..	..	(25·9)	(7·2)	(6·7)	(7·4)	(7·3)
Consumers' goods	..	..	4·8	15·2	18·3	20·6	23·9

B. Commodities

		1938	1950	1955	1957	1958
Coal and coke	⎫	neg.	8800	9114	3794	5504
Oil and oil products		141	2613	4390	4268	4296
Rolling mill products		88	185	86	723	784
Pipes		24	n.a.	123	123	158
Copper			On secret list *			
Lead		42	16	18	28	30
Tin		11	5	17	22	19
Natural rubber		n.a.	n.a.	35	146	259
Raw cotton		16	45	20	109	142
Raw wool	⎬ (000 tons)	29	35	46	57	55
Raw tobacco		neg.	38	55	91	84
Soya beans		0	500	484	579	478
Cocoa beans		15	12	14	44	10
Tea		17	6	10	21	26
Meat & meat products		3	47	239	117	157
Fish & fish products		14	30	117	122	110
Rice		40	40	488	371	501
Sugar, refined		0	358	728	294	181
Sugar, raw		0	0	206	351	198
Fresh fruit	⎭	34	3	133	218	335
Wool fabrics (m. metres)		neg.	n.a.	11	15	14
Clothing (m. of roubles)		neg.	n.a.	90	602	886

* The Russians do not reveal the details for 'strategic' reasons.

Sources: *Narodnoe Khozyaistvo SSSR v 1958 godu*, pp. 800-804, and Soviet trade returns.

B. East German External Trade

TABLE I, BY GROUPS OF COUNTRIES

	1955 IMPORTS	1955 EXPORTS	1956 IMPORTS	1956 EXPORTS	1957 IMPORTS	1957 EXPORTS	1958 IMPORTS	1958 EXPORTS
*With Soviet bloc (mill. D.M.)	1841	2090	2141	2317	2570	3022	2647	3223
(mill. Roubles)	3313	3761	3853	4171	4626	5438	4765	5802
With rest of world (mill. D.M.)	474	448	498	468	612	548	663	507
(mill. Roubles)	854	806	897	843	1101	986	1194	912
Inter-German trade (mill. D.M.)	291	303	325	342	409	455	423	469
(mill. Roubles)	524	546	585	616	736	819	761	845
TOTAL (mill. D.M.) ..	2606	2840	2964	3127	3590	4024	3733	4199
(mill. Roubles) ..	4691	5113	5335	5629	6462	7244	6720	7559

* Including Yugoslavia.
Sources: *Statistisches Jahrbuch*, 1957, 1958 *Statistik* Quarterly, No. 1/1959, p.20.

TABLE II, BY COUNTRY
(excluding trade with West Germany)

(Millions of Roubles—180 Roubles=100 D.M. after 1954)

	1955 IMPORTS	1955 EXPORTS	1956 IMPORTS	1956 EXPORTS	1957 IMPORTS	1957 EXPORTS	1958 IMPORTS	1958 EXPORTS
BLOC COUNTRIES								
Albania :: :: ::	5	25	8	18	11	18	11	24
Bulgaria :: :: ::	124	85	137	130	106	119	121	146
China :: :: ::	347	390	344	380	354	423	415	533

Czechoslovakia .. : : :	603	567	562	476	439	421	375	283
Hungary .. : : :	245	283	253	188	191	157	184	248
Mongolia .. : : :	11	7	5	7	0	—	—	0
North Korea : : :	22	11	27	10	33	7	30	—
North Vietnam : : :	20	17	17	10	19	1	7	—
Poland .. : : :	575	339	604	412	556	419	495	459
Rumania .. : : :	138	121	136	84	114	117	99	152
USSR .. : : :	3,384	2,777	3,239	2,944	2,277	2,228	2,063	1,688
TOTAL BLOC COUNTRIES ..	5,701	4,669	5,403	4,602	4,157	3,839	3,753	3,306
REST OF THE WORLD								
Belgium and Luxembourg ..	44	59	39	33	32	46	25	46
Denmark .. : :	57	53	51	40	56	55	56	60
United Kingdom .. :	49	134	60	132	49	70	48	70
Finland .. : :	45	56	86	64	81	70	79	69
France .. : :	34	66	31	67	16	37	17	30
Holland .. : :	61	88	85	81	85	108	73	117
Yugoslavia .. :	101	96	35	24	13	14	8	7
Norway .. : :	27	30	27	33	40	31	29	33
Austria .. : :	55	61	54	57	42	65	53	52
Sweden .. : :	51	56	52	58	58	49	55	52
India .. : :	37	27	29	31	23	14	13	5
Turkey .. : :	85	67	73	66	54	63	57	47
Egypt .. : :	100	99	93	69	32	38	25	18
Brazil .. : :	4	50	7	34	2	15	2	0
USA .. : :	24	23	24	14	28	24	29	21
TOTAL REST OF THE WORLD ..	1,012	1,290	1,021	1,124	856	911	814	860
TOTAL ALL COUNTRIES ..	6,713	5,959	6,424	5,726	5,013	4,750	4,567	4,166

Source: *Statistisches Jahrbuch, 1957, 1958*

95

B. East German External Trade

TABLE III, BY COMMODITY

EXPORTS*

		1955	1956	1957	1958
Electrical energy (mill. Kwh.)		220	273	359	313
Coal (brown)		5219	4462	4753	6190
Sodium sulphate		173	197	203	192
Potash (Na$_2$Co$_3$)	(000 tons)	78	84	110	104
Petrol		183	152	128	76
Diesel oil		274	206	299	276
Cement		685	570	199	189
Tiles (000 units)		3502	4977	3208	1695
Lathes		840	1539	1144	1092
Engines (petrol)		1022	4398	7590	3138
Steam locomotives		15	43	6	—
Electric locomotives		179	119	154	1414
Passenger wagons		561	606	830	946
Goods wagons	(units)	1659	1649	836	665
Passenger cars		8525	11214	12742	12566
Commercial vehicles including Mopeds		8657	25661	47806	59900
Household appliances		73012	103843	109399	101000
Electric motors		9043	15923	11410	20184
Typewriters (office)		21772	23592	27458	32800
„ (portable)		93041	115865	104506	133100
Watches and clocks (000 units)		1294	1428	1497	1648
Cameras (000 units)		210	231	266	212
Textiles—fibre (000 sq. m.)		2400	6051	8347	8569
Cotton—fabrics (000 sq. m.)		5369	8818	13743	10417
Sugar (000 tons)		127	75	50	168
Wheat		8278	556	1334	1200
Rye	(tons)	29728	102672	1841	n.a.
Barley		—	86178	1682	n.a.
TOTAL (mill. Rbl.)		5113	5629	7243	7559
(mill. D.M.)		2841	3128	4024	4199

Source: Statistisches Jahrbuch—1957, 1958

*Machinery and equipment account for the greater part of East German exports to the Soviet bloc. Full statistics on machinery are not available.

B. East German External Trade

TABLE III, BY COMMODITY

IMPORTS*

		1955	1956	1957	1958
Electrical energy (mill. Kwh.)		212	127	29	19
Gas (mill. cubic m.)		91	101	128	99
Coal (hard)		6338	5641	5753	7397
Coke		2613	2271	2689	2452
Cast iron		100	141	174	169
Steel	(000 tons)	194	204	270	388
Steel-mill products		651	789	931	1155
Natural rubber		10	10	16	17
Ground-nut oil		648	798	997	1127
Phosphates		50	60	59	62
Passenger cars (units)		433	1300	1436	11429
Sawn wood (000 cubic m.)		214	299	644	737
Cotton fabrics (000 sq. m.)		39450	21108	17898	33100
Leather shoes (000 pairs)		1047	510	788	1453
Wood pulp		13·4	23·3	35·7	43·3
Paper		18·0	15·4	16·6	20·9
Meat & meat products		89	96	114	63
Vegetable oil		61	85	71	85
Butter	(000 tons)	15	30	37	22
Wheat		555	606	1078	1292
Rye		187	482	342	207
Barley		440	365	387	85
Rice		78	54	63	59
TOTAL (mill. Roubles)		4691	5335	6462	6720
(million DM)		2606	2964	3590	3733

Source: *Statistisches Jahrbuch*, 1957, 1958

* Fuel, raw materials and consumer goods account for approximately 90 per cent of East German total imports.

97

C. Polish External Trade TABLE I, BY COUNTRY (millions of Zloty)

(1 zloty dewizowe=1 Rouble=$0.25=1s. 10d.)

	1955 IMPORTS	1955 EXPORTS	1956 IMPORTS	1956 EXPORTS	1957 IMPORTS	1957 EXPORTS	1958 IMPORTS	1958 EXPORTS
BLOC COUNTRIES								
Albania	n.a.	n.a.	5	8	8	13	8	18
Bulgaria	28	38	42	26	59	48	75	69
Czechoslovakia	319	301	412	305	309	244	378	290
China	141	140	141	201	149	179	145	289
East Germany	487	500	541	430	660	501	597	426
Hungary	122	106	92	99	83	130	135	115
North Korea	n.a.	n.a.	5	53	11	14	3	7
North Vietnam	n.a.	n.a.	3	13	13	6	14	14
Rumania	48	50	57	77	62	68	49	54
USSR	1,254	1,122	1,377	1082	1,688	1,034	1,336	1,061
TOTAL BLOC COUNTRIES	(2,399)¹	(2,257)¹	2,675	2,294	3,042	2,233	2,735	2,343
REST OF THE WORLD								
Belgium	48	16	44	28	56	21	67	25
Finland	62	131	71	134	99	170	83	80
France	138	51	129	124	91	161	109	81
Yugoslavia	n.a.	n.a.	36	29	71	73	89	136
West Germany	94	118	226	212	221	200	269	284
Holland	n.a.	n.a.	69	31	107	18	54	30
Austria	71	114	107	97	139	127	140	109
Switzerland	n.a.	n.a.	66	40	44	40	47	57
Sweden	60	83	60	106	86	65	93	56
Egypt	n.a.	n.a.	20	19	70	28	50	45
United Kingdom	167	312	131	317	189	255	332	275
Brazil	n.a.	n.a.	31	52	67	51	67	67
USA	n.a.	n.a.	10	95	223	107	407	107
Argentine	–	–	–	–	21	11	69	72
Spain	–	–	–	–	3	4	25	21
TOTAL REST OF THE WORLD	(1,328)¹	(1,397)¹	1,412	1,605	1,964	1,667	2,172	1,895
TOTAL ALL COUNTRIES	3,727	3,654	4,087	3,899	5,006	3,900	4,907	4,238

Sources: For 1958—*Biuletyn Statystyczny*, No. 2/1959, p. 28. ¹ Figures in brackets are approximate.
—*Rocznik Statystyczny*—1957 *and* 1958.

C. Polish External Trade

TABLE II, BY COMMODITY

EXPORTS

(at 1956 prices)

			1955	1956	1957	1958*
I. Machinery, equipment and transport (million zloty)			490	616	780	1137
including						
Locomotives	⎫	(units)	237	232	243	27
Goods wagons	⎬		2792	4535	3070	4118
Passenger wagons	⎭		277	312	485	469
Ships (000 zloty)			148391	151672	169800	232800
II. Raw and other materials (million zloty)			2713	2511	2021	2154
including						
Coal (hard)	⎫		24146	19187	13357	16204
Coke	⎬	(000 tons)	2240	2283	1925	2069
Rolled products			225	466	559	593
Zinc and zinc plates	⎭		96	96	92	86
Wood pulp (000 cu. metres)			492	440	287	131
III. Agricultural consumer goods (million zloty)			580	460	511	714
including						
Meat & meat products	⎫	(000 tons)	73	88	88	91
Sugar	⎭		372	61	98	222
Eggs (million units)			344	343	360	396
IV. Industrial consumer goods (million zloty)			252	351	273	232
including						
Cotton fabrics	⎫	(000	57466	92734	63750	25912
Woollen fabrics	⎭	metres)	5780	7229	3897	3262
TOTAL (million zloty)			4035	3939	3586	4238

*at current prices.

Sources: *Rocznik Statystycnzy,* 1957, 1958, 1959
Biuletyn Statystyczny, No. 2/1959, p. 29.

C. Polish External Trade

TABLE II, BY COMMODITY

IMPORTS

(at 1956 prices)

		1955	1956	1957	1958*
I. Machinery, equipment and transport (mill. zloty) including		1648	1358	1190	1310
Equipment for complete factories		363	211	192	123
Electrical and power equipment	(mill. zloty)	158	140	111	166
Agricultural machinery and equipment		64	72	65	33
II. Raw and other materials (million zloty) including		1936	1987	2513	2648
Oil		545	537	630	600
Oil products		886	952	1134	1274
Iron ore		4407	4776	5914	5750
Zinc concentrates		80	91	152	107
Natural and synthetic rubber	(000 tons)	26	34	43	49
Cotton		95	86	121	105
Wool		16	16	19	32
Fertilizers		1293	1408	1512	1248
III. Agricultural products (million zloty) including		464	506	768	539
Wheat		739	664	1794	666
Rye	(000 tons)	415	309	—	210
Maize		7	27	12	56
Rice		31	32	28	28
IV. Industrial consumer goods (million zloty) including		160	236	304	410
Textiles (million zloty)		22	54	56	n.a.
Leather footwear (000 pairs)		1050	1418	1077	3109
Bicycles	(000 units)	—	194	257	n.a.
Radio sets		—	43	80	n.a.
TOTAL (mill. zloty)		4208	4087	4775	4907

* At current prices.

Sources: *Rocznik Statystyczny*, 1957, 1958, 1959
Biuletyn Statystyczny, No. 2/1959. p. 29.

100

D. Czechoslovakian External Trade

TABLE 1, BY GROUPS OF COUNTRIES
(*Indices:* 1948=100)

	1955	1956	1957	1958*
IMPORTS—Total	175·7	197·5	232·8	227·8
with : Soviet bloc	313·1	328·8	408·7	398·5
Other countries	83·7	109·5	114·8	113·3
EXPORTS—Total	227·4	269·3	270·9	301·9
with : Soviet bloc	329·3	369·3	374·5	450·0
Other countries	135·4	179·0	177·4	170·5

Source :
Statistická Ročenka Republiky Ceskoslovenské, 1958, p. 315.

* Computed from data given in *Statistické Zpravy—Rok* 1959, pp. 17-18.

D. Czechoslovakian External Trade   TABLE II, BY COUNTRY

(Millions of Kčs)
20.2 Kčs=£1

	1955		1956		1957		1958	
	IMPORTS	EXPORTS	IMPORTS	EXPORTS	IMPORTS	EXPORTS	IMPORTS	EXPORTS
BLOC COUNTRIES								
Albania	14	41	24	36	33	43	30	69
Bulgaria	175	312	229	259	341	243	298	261
China	437	415	478	466	482	585	655	786
East Germany	705	574	851	1,010	1,039	952	1,167	1,134
Hungary	555	461	467	424	528	547	651	557
Mongolia	—	—	—	—	9	14	21	30
North Korea	1	34	6	90	8	122	11	85
North Vietnam	—	30	32	45	37	29	22	32
Poland	548	740	554	714	432	563	515	683
Rumania	300	270	205	252	192	267	161	272
USSR	2,631	2,900	2,808	3,085	3,856	2,866	3,253	3,579
TOTAL BLOC COUNTRIES	5,366	5,777	5,654	6,381	6,957	6,231	6,784	7,488
REST OF THE WORLD								
Belgium and Luxembourg	57	61	91	83	81	81	102	72
Finland	59	130	80	157	96	166	74	59
France	53	51	91	64	92	107	128	127
Yugoslavia	53	44	48	97	42	135	108	180
West Germany	119	224	280	364	431	395	445	386
Holland	88	119	135	133	159	125	114	102
Austria	120	135	155	144	180	148	150	140
Switzerland	144	139	207	153	171	160	197	172
United Kingdom	202	163	193	178	261	248	233	211
Egypt and Syria	151	83	241	72	199	174	277	328
Brazil	155	162	144	145	116	98	114	105
USA	4	25	5	39	10	44	7	54
TOTAL REST OF THE WORLD	2,213	2,690	2,883	3,607	3,028	3,545	2,988	3,407
TOTAL ALL COUNTRIES	7,579	8,467	8,537	9,988	9,985	9,776	9,772	10,895

Source: *Statistická Ročenka Republiky Československé—1958*, p. 316; 1958 *Statistické Zpravy—Rok* 1959 No. 8 pp. 17 and 18.

D. Czechoslovakian External Trade

TABLE III, BY COMMODITY

EXPORTS

	1955	1956	1957	1958
I. Machines, equipment and tools (mill. Kcs.)	3680	4022	3993	4725
including				
Metal-working machines	5489	7911	8481	10579
Lorries	2527	2486	2602	4829
Passenger cars (units)	9441	14718	15858	25037
Motorcycles	32423	51183	80119	109053
Tractors	8865	9888	14445	15192
II. Fuels, materials and raw materials (mill. Kcs.)	3325	3688	3404	3391
including				
Coke (000 tons)	1198	1256	1159	1045
Sawn wood (000 cubic m.)	563	427	576	616
Paper (000 tons)	59	56	63	66
Plate glass (000 sq. m.) ..	12521	12579	11715	12247
Coal (brown-lignite) (000 tons)	1177	1273	1540	1266
III. Livestock for breeding and other live animals (mill. Kcs.)	3	3	6	6
IV. Foodstuffs, including raw materials (mill. Kcs.)	519	739	675	769
including				
Malt (000 tons)	123	133	143	143
Beer (000hl.)	212	226	247	370
V. Non-food consumer goods (mill. Kcs.)	940	1536	1698	2004
including				
Cotton fabrics	81751	123792	126516	116144
Silk fabrics (000 m.)	1788	7191	8311	8812
Linen fabrics	5961	14097	14664	14333
Leather shoes (000 pairs)	2761	12080	10492	14030
Rubber shoes (000 pairs)	9977	13949	13216	13851
TOTAL (mill. Kcs.)	8467	9988	9776	10895

Sources:
Statistická Ročenka Republiky Ceskoslovenské—1958 pp. 315-319.
and 1959 p. 362
1958 *Statistické Zpravy Rok* 1959, No. 8, p. 20.

D. Czechoslovakian External Trade

TABLE III, BY COMMODITY

IMPORTS

	1955	1956	1957	1958
I. Machines, equipment and tools (mill. Kcs.)	1005	1465	1872	1825
II. Fuels, materials and raw materials (mill. Kcs.) ..	4064	4699	5393	5348
including				
Oil & oil products (000 tons) ..	1060	1176	1609	1645
Iron ore (000 tons)	3926	3903	4923	5163
Phosphates (P₂0₅) (000 tons) ..	100	92	96	122
Coal (000 tons)	4066	3451	2251	2576
Rubber (natural) (000 tons) ..	30	38	44	49
Fertiliser (potash) (000 tons) ..	158	168	187	217
III. Livestock (mill. Kcs.) ..	2	4	5	3
IV. Foodstuffs, including raw materials (mill. Kcs.) ..	2196	2100	2322	2259
including				
Wheat (000 tons)	816	661	974	964
*((grain) (000 tons)	871	742	1036)	
Barley fodder (000 tons) ..	261	371	236	88
Meat (000 tons)	77	55	54	92
Fish (000 tons)	44	41	40	43
Eggs (mill.)	60	63	36	57
Rice (000 tons)	40	57	81	74
Fruit (000 tons)	133	110	106	116
Vegetables (000 tons)	46	57	92	63
V. Non-food consumer goods (mill. Kcs.)	312	269	393	337
including				
Passenger cars (units)	1476	5620	10549	9538
Television sets	—	14200	73720	51773
TOTAL (mill. Kcs)	7579	8537	9985	9772

Sources:
Statistická Ročenka Republiky Ceskoslovenské—1958, pp. 315-319,
and 1959 pp. 362-367.
1958 *Statistické Zpravy Rok* 1959, No. 8, p. 19.

* Czechoslovak *Statistical Abstract*—1958, p.19.

Book II
The Mechanics of East-West Trade

Part I
The Background

THE AUTHOR

Desmond Donnelly has been MP for Pembrokeshire since 1950. He is well known for his writings, lectures and broadcasts on a wide range of topics, and for his travels behind the Iron Curtain which he discussed in a recent book, *The March Wind*. His longest visits were in 1952, 1954 and 1957, when he went as far as Siberia and China.

CHAPTER I

Problems of Trading with Communists

1. Introduction

There are four different types of Communist country. It is essential to draw the distinction between them—whether our dealings with them are political or economic.

First, there is the Soviet Union, which retains the economic leadership of the Communist bloc, and is likely to do so for at least another generation.

Secondly, there are the East European Communist countries, whose political and economic patterns were laid down in the early years of Communist Government in each of these countries—a period coinciding with the last years of Stalin's life.

Thirdly, there is China—moulded by the new revolution. In China the climate for trade—and indeed, the pattern of it—is analogous to the early period following the revolution in Russia. Some of the suspicions and inexperience, and much of the excessive centralisation associated with the Soviet Union in the nineteen thirties, are to be found in the China of the early nineteen sixties.

Finally, outside the Soviet bloc, but still Communist in background and thought, is Jugoslavia. In Jugoslavia, the system is more elastic, but is still basically formulated by a central state plan. It is significant, however, that as time passes and Stalinism recedes, the other European Communist countries will begin to eye these developments in Jugoslavia—indeed in some instances, they are

107

already overhauling the start Jugoslavia made in liberalisation following her break with the Soviet bloc in 1948.

Despite the differences in post-war Communist development, economic circumstances, and, of course, geography that make for these four different types of Communist country, there are certain features common to all: chiefly, that they are all planned economies. The corollary is that *all* foreign trade has to fit into each national economic plan; and the prospects for trade outside these economic plans are very restricted indeed. To that extent, any western business man or manufacturer seeking to promote trade with the Communist bloc must acquaint himself thoroughly with the pattern of the economy into which he aims to break. He must study the basic structure of that country's industrial and agricultural policy. For so tightly-knit are these Communist patterns that there is little, if any, opportunity for the individualist or for the type of trading adventurer who is traditional in our national commerce. That is not to say that there is no chance for initiative from the West in East-West trade. In a sense there is all the more need for it. But it is no use trying to exercise it without being fully aware of the deliberately built and politically motivated structure which must be scaled with knowledge and precision if East-West trade is to be conducted with mutual benefit and profit.

2. *Foreign trade within the Soviet bloc*

Foreign trade within the whole Soviet bloc is secondary to the general drive for self-sufficiency within the bloc as a comprehensive unit or economic empire. The foreign trade of each unit of the bloc therefore is fitted, as a piece in a mosaic, into the pattern of the bloc as a whole. It is important, therefore, to examine more closely the process by which all the Communist economies are integrated.

This integration is organised by *Comecon*, the bloc's Council of Mutual Economic Assistance.

Comecon was founded in January 1949, as a counter to the Marshall Plan, which in the first place had attracted several East European countries. The founder members of *Comecon* were Soviet Russia, Poland, Hungary, Czechoslovakia, Bulgaria and Roumania. Later, they were joined by East Germany and Albania. After 1953, China, Outer Mongolia, North Korea and North Viet Nam were admitted as observers. At certain moments of rapprochement, Jugoslavia has also attended sessions of *Comecon*.

The original terms of reference of *Comecon* were 'to strengthen the economic collaboration of the Socialist countries and to co-ordinate their economic development on the basis of equal rights of all member states by organising the exchange of economic and technical experience and rendering mutual aid in raw materials, food and equipment.'* In the first phase, *Comecon* limited its activities to trade relations; there was little interest in production problems. During this early period, *Comecon* also served the immediate reconstruction of the Soviet Union. Partly because of the revaluation of the rouble in 1950 and also because of arbitrary price fixing determined in Moscow, the countries of eastern Europe found themselves at a great disadvantage as compared with the Soviet Union. Production and trade were treated as instruments of the declared policy of self-sufficiency. As a consequence, by 1953, four-fifths of the total exports of individual Communist countries had become transactions within the bloc. Trade with the rest of the world had dwindled to insignificance.

After Stalin's death, a new and more flexible *Comecon* policy was adopted. Reparations were ended; and, for the first time, export prices were based on those of the world commodity markets. Simultaneously, there was severe criticism within the Soviet bloc of the duplication of the industrial efforts among its members. This led to *Comecon* being given the task of co-ordinating economic planning in the interests of the bloc as a whole, rather than of its individual members.

In 1956, some twelve standing commissions of *Comecon* were created to deal with different aspects of the economic activity of the entire Soviet bloc. Provision was made for the co-ordination of production and of raw material supplies. At the same time, priorities of production were laid down among *Comecon's* members. These priorities were based largely on existing industrial patterns. They were not arbitrary. They took note of national susceptibilities. But there were certain restrictions on production and allocation of materials. In the result, the following priorities were agreed upon:

1. Eastern Germany—precision instruments, electrical equipment.
2. Poland—rolling stock, mining equipment.

* Vneshnaya Torgovlya SSSR s Sotsialisticheskimi Stranami, Moscow 1957.

3. Czechoslovakia—motor cars, engines.

4. Hungary—diesel engines, lorries.

5. Roumania—oil pipes, drilling equipment.

A decade had passed since *Comecon* was founded. In that period, its work had proved of such value to the economic development of the whole Soviet Communist and satellite economy, that it was obvious that from this point onwards *Comecon* must become an increasingly important factor. Its Council decided to base itself on longer-range plans, covering ten to fifteen years. They fixed a meeting of political heads, which was held in Moscow in May 1958. Among other things, this meeting decided upon the construction of the major Soviet pipeline to Europe.

Since the second decade opened, *Comecon* has been charged with the duty of making more rapid progress towards its declared goal of economic integration of the Communist bloc. For instance, the Eleventh Session held in Tirana (May 1959) dealt with practical matters including bottlenecks in the supply of vital products such as steel castings. A long-term scheme to co-ordinate the electric grids of the *Comecon* countries was also approved.

From all this, it is clear that plans for economic integration within the Communist bloc are now much further advanced than ever before. The machinery of economic integration certainly exists; but it has still to prove that the processes it has established will work better than a freer economy would have done.

If *Comecon* should prove more successful, it may lead to greater self-sufficiency within the bloc—and in consequence, to a lessening of East-West trade in the years following 1965. But, even if *Comecon* should succeed beyond the dreams of its creators, there is still the unforeseeable political factor that may undermine or upset all the most careful economic calculations. No one at this moment can forecast how East-West political relations will stand by that same date.

Outside the framework of *Comecon*, China and Russia entered into a major trade agreement in 1959 which served to bind the bloc yet closer. By this agreement, in scope and substance much greater than any of its predecessors, the Soviet Union committed itself to long-term credits to facilitate Chinese industrial expansion. In return, China committed her future agricultural production to help to pay for the industrial goods that are to come from Russia under the agreement.

This brief introduction to the practical trading arrangements within the Communist bloc shows clearly that, in contrast with Britain, the Communist countries regard trade with the non-Communist world as the marginal residual of the Communist economy. Furthermore, when Communist leaders speak of 'foreign trade' they often mean foreign trade within the bloc. This is an extremely important point for westerners to grasp.

A statement like this does not mean that trade between the West and the Communist countries is impossible. On the contrary, the figures show (see Book I Part III, A) that there has been a steady expansion in foreign trade since Stalin's death. And, as stated earlier, despite the declared prospect of *Comecon*, it is possible that further political changes in both East and West may lead to yet more trade developments in the future. I refer again later to these speculations.

Two factors give rise to this hope.

The first is the growing demand for consumer goods in the more advanced Communist countries. It is not likely that there will be an extensive consumer goods trade between East and West for some time. But because of the demand, the Communist planners are faced with the prospect of either permitting adequate imports to meet the need (with the counter-balancing trade in the other direction, according to the Communist method) or of shifting their internal economic plan to provide more consumer goods from within their own productive capacity. Such a shift would be a considerable strain on their internal economic effort, and in itself might call for imports from the West to meet it. In either case, the internal demand for more consumer goods is a factor to be considered, and to be studied seriously by western manufacturers and traders.

This switch in the internal economic pattern of the Communist bloc was pointed out in the United Nations *Economic Bulletin for Europe*, 1959, which underlined this point in graphic form: 'The most striking common feature of the plans of all the eastern European countries is the substantial increase in the rate of fixed capital formation everywhere intended in 1959, in marked contrast to the policies of the recent past'.

Secondly, as the Soviet Union and the more industrialised countries of the bloc begin to find themselves with a greater volume of exportable products, the trade from the bloc to the outside world will grow. Trade has to be a two-way affair, which will mean eventually that the Communist countries will have to import in order to export —a logic that should not escape western business men who still seek only to sell and not to buy.

3. *The strategic embargo*

One of the problems of any western business man seeking to trade with the Communist bloc comes not from the East, but from the West—the system of embargo on the export from the West of goods on the strategic embargo list. The system is based on the security control which began to operate in 1947, after the outbreak of the Cold War. The list is drawn up in association by the leading western nations, although the American list is much longer than that of the European countries; and so far as China is concerned, for political reasons, the United States has deliberately restricted trade of all kinds as far as possible. In the past, this has led to two different lists in Britain, one for China and another for the rest of the Soviet bloc; it has also led to differences within the Anglo-American alliance, but that is another story.

The difficulties of enforcing the embargo have been considerable. Clearly, there could be no final check that goods exported to a neutral country were not re-exported to a Communist country; or that goods legitimately exported to a Communist country on the European list were not then transferred to China—that goods exported legally to Hungary for example, were not re-exported from there to Peking though they would originally have been on the embargo list of western or British goods to China. In fact, this is exactly how the Communist countries have evaded the embargo; and Communist officials have made no secret about it in conversations that I have had in the various capitals of the bloc. To give one illustration: I once saw a large consignment of embargoed Ford trucks being unpacked near Peking. When I enquired at the Ministry of Foreign Trade how these embargoed goods got there, I was told frankly that the vehicles had been ordered direct from the Ford Motor Company in the United States by a purchasing agent of the Chinese Communist Government living in Switzerland.

These days, the embargo list published by the Board of Trade is the same for the Communist bloc as a whole; no distinction is drawn between China and the other Communist countries. The list is drawn up under the overall control of *Cocom* (the Committee of the Paris Consultative Group). This is a body which, in practice, consists of the member states of the North Atlantic Treaty Alliance (excluding Iceland) and Japan, which has substantial trade with the Communist bloc. Each member state is responsible for its own administration of the agreed international list, which is considered as the accepted minimum—and which is published periodically in the *Board of Trade Journal*.

4. *Contract terms*

Efficient Communist planning depends on precise delivery dates. That is why East-West trade contracts often seem to us in the West unduly meticulous as regards penalties and safeguards. Further, again because Communist planning cannot afford any slip-up, their contracts take particular heed of travel risks over the long distances involved: proper packaging guarantees are also essential to safeguard the exporter's interests, for one set of cautions demands another.

In the case of capital goods, most Communist countries insist on inspection clauses. The Soviet Union is particularly emphatic on this point, and it is useful to have competent interpreters on hand to avoid misunderstanding, for these inspections can be thorough and demanding.

There is one advantage, however, in trading with a Communist country—for as the contract is in effect made with the Government, there are very few cases of payments defaulting! Most contracts should be regarded as honourable documents. For United Kingdom exports, payment in the past has been, as a rule, made against shipping documents, or within 30 days of shipment; but of late, credit terms have been more and more an accepted practice. This last point is particularly true of those Communist countries that have continual balance of payments problems.

For United Kingdom imports, the same terms broadly apply.

The Export Credits Guarantee Department of the British Government is prepared to extend normal cover to transactions with nearly all the Communist countries and restricted cover to only a few.

Should any dispute arise, arbitration is a continual problem. So far as Russia is concerned, business men with experience have described the procedure as fair; it is usually possible to arrive at a

H

compromise between London and Moscow, with arbitration conducted in a neutral country. As far as China and the other Communist countries are concerned, the position is less satisfactory at the time of writing. In China particularly, arbitration facilities are inadequate; exporters should take great care, therefore, to ensure that the circumstances that give rise to arbitration do not arise.*

Patents and designs can also lead to trouble. Because they must build up their industries as rapidly as possible, Communist countries have made free use of western designs. They do not necessarily regard this as any infringement. Because of their ideologies, Communist governments tend to take a different view from the rest of the world of what the West accepts as proprietorial rights. To date, they are unwilling to concede that large quantities of capital are necessary to develop new products; and that in order to develop yet newer products, recoupment is essential.

With this problem in mind, a mission visited Moscow in late 1959, led by the Comptroller General of the Patent Office. Whilst certain difficulties remain, the Soviet authorities claim that the new Soviet Patent Law can be used to protect western patents, *provided that these are registered in the Soviet Union.* The recommendation of the British Mission is that British industry should explore the practical working of this law and comply with the Soviet suggestion that in future appropriate British patents should be registered simultaneously in London and Moscow.

5. *Advertising*

There is a general and misguided belief in the West that in Communist countries there is no advertising; that because imports of Communist countries are planned, advertising is of no value. This is not necessarily true. Whilst trade has to go through the approved channels of the Ministries of Foreign Trade, the original demand for goods often originates much further down at factory manager level.

---

* In cases of difficulty, advice can be obtained from the following: Federation of British Industries, 21, Tothill Street, London, SW1; London Chamber of Commerce, (Russian Section), 69 Cannon Street, London, EC4; The Russo-British Chamber of Commerce, 2, Lowndes Square, London, SW1; The China Association, Broad Street House, 54 Old Broad Street, London, EC2; or any of the other principal chambers of commerce.

When I was in Moscow in 1957, I saw a new British cigarette manufacturing machine being unpacked at a cigarette factory. The factory director pointed it out to me with great pride. Why had he ordered this particular model, I asked, and not a comparable machine from some other manufacturer or country? He explained that he had visited Britain on a trade delegation and had seen the machine working at the Players' Factory at Nottingham. On his return to Russia he had asked if he could have a similar machine for his own factory. His request had gone first to the Moscow *Sovnarkhoz* and after approval, at district level, it had eventually passed through the processes of *Gosplan* and reached the Ministry of Foreign Trade. In its turn, the Ministry of Foreign Trade had instructed the appropriate importing organisation to open negotiations for the purchase of the machine. The whole process had taken about two years—a long time, but the point is nevertheless clear: sometimes it is the demand at factory level that wins a place in the overall plan. In short, the factory director in a Communist country can be as vulnerable to an impression as can any potential purchaser anywhere. It is therefore well worth propagating western goods—though it may sometimes be longer than two years before an order develops.

Advertising is clearly the one practical means of reaching the person who can stimulate such a demand, and who is not fortunate enough to visit the West as a privileged member of a delegation. Apart from the details set out under the relevant chapters later, there is a Russian language technical journal published in Britain and circulated to factory directors and *Sovnarkhozi* in the Soviet Union under the title *British Industry and Engineering*.*

6. *Conclusion*

There *are* potentialities for expanding trade with the Communist bloc. But that trade is conditioned by politics. The main limitation on trade is imposed by political decision—the declared Communist aim that the bloc is striving to achieve economic self-sufficiency. The range of products in which it is possible to promote increases in trade is, therefore, limited.

The techniques of East-West trade are different from the normally accepted practices between countries outside the bloc. Each East-West transaction has to be fitted into the national economic pattern

* The editorial offices are at Walker House, Bedford Street, London, WC2.

of the Communist countries concerned, and before any contract is signed, it has to pass the scrutiny of the economic planners. The principles of free trade, as the West knows them, just do not apply.

The task of stimulating trade is therefore infinitely greater—and different. Some trade is promoted on the basis that the Communist country requires a particular product that is unobtainable within the bloc. Thereby, enquiries are initiated and after the relevant production Ministry has sponsored the demand and it has been passed by the economic planning authority, the order goes via the Ministry of Foreign Trade to the appropriate state trading corporation. Thereupon, the state trading corporation asks for quotations in the countries in which it is regarded as politically desirable that the purchase should be made. When quotations have been considered, priced and decided upon at this level, the order is signed.

That is one way. The other way is for the western business man to initiate the transaction himself by stimulating the interest of the Communist purchaser. The recognised method here is to approach the relevant state trading organisation or its agents direct, relying upon those bodies to make known the qualities of the product offered for sale.

An even more determined trader might supplement this action by attempting to reach the Communist executive who was actually responsible for using the product. This is possible. But it can be done only by personal visits, by personal return invitations, and by the use of advertising, as I have outlined.

If there is to be any substantial East-West trade, this last method is the only way. To accept the normal formula is not enough—any more than it is in promoting trade anywhere. The Communist Iron Curtain must be pushed hard, and every device known to traders down the centuries must be exercised.

The purpose of my contribution is to indicate some of the ways and means by which these additional approaches can be made; and to try to provide a thread through the political maze of Communist countries in which East-West trade is otherwise completely lost.

CHAPTER II

The Soviet Union

1. *Background*

The first Anglo-Russian trade agreement was signed by Richard Chancellor in 1553. Since then, trade between the two countries has undergone many vicissitudes. There is nothing new about the fact that Russian buying policies sometimes appear to be shaped by political considerations. For the Russian practice of using trade as a political weapon goes back for at least two hundred years.

The modern background to Soviet trade originates in the situation prevailing immediately after the Russian revolution. At that time a large amount of foreign assets in Russia (including substantial British holdings) had been seized by the Bolsheviks. As a result, foreign relations were extremely bad. The intervention of the Western powers in the Russian Civil War added to the existing open hostility and led to yet further reprisals. It was therefore some time before the new rulers of Russia began to establish trade relations with the outside world. So far as Britain was concerned, the first important steps were taken during the period of the first Labour Government of 1923-4.

Following the recognition by Britain of the new Soviet regime, a permanent Soviet trade delegation under the name of Arcos was established in London. Certain British firms with products that were relevant to Soviet needs also began to establish contacts. Anglo-Soviet trade suffered a major setback in 1927, however, when officials of Arcos were accused of association with an espionage network; and Anglo-Soviet diplomatic relations were severed again for a time.

Eventually more regular relations were established. Despite such setbacks as the so-called 'Metrovick trials', trade tended to adhere

117

to the established pattern up to the outbreak of the Cold War, when, for a time, there was a sharp falling off.

The turning point came with the Moscow Economic Conference of 1952, significantly while Stalin was still alive. Since then, there has been a steady increase in the volume of trade. The circumstances that led up to this point need brief examination, for they are part of the psychology of modern Russia.

The death of Stalin was an event of profound importance in the Communist world. He had dominated the scene for so long that his word had eventually become law; and if this had not been sufficient, his authority was also backed by the largest apparatus of secret police in the history of the world. During the early years of Stalin's ascendancy, the Soviet Union passed through periods of social disruption and upheaval. Millions died from starvation in the early 1930's. When, in the late 1930's, Stalin sought to divert attention from the country's internal problems by creating a fiction of foreign threats, millions more were imprisoned or executed. There was a period when almost every foreigner in the Soviet Union was labelled a potential spy or saboteur.

Estimates vary, and there can be no certainty, but upwards of five million Russians, nearly all of them innocent, suffered denunciation and deportation to slave labour camps in the more remote regions of the Soviet Union. Hysteria reached such a point that each unit of administration was given a *norm* of denunciations to fulfil each month.

Where all this would have led if Hitler had not invaded Russia in 1941, it is impossible to tell. But it was the Nazi invasion, more than any other event, that united the Russian nation behind its Communist leadership. Even then, the outcome of the Communist Revolution was in doubt. There were riots in Moscow when the German army reached the City's suburbs and many Communists tore up their party cards. The Soviet Government, without Stalin, fled to Kubyshev. And then the news was whispered around that Stalin was still in the Kremlin. Stalin remained in the Kremlin; and it was in the setting of those towers and minarets that he grew to be the great war leader and world figure that history will regard him. He became the personification of Russian resistance to the invader. He revealed an amazing grasp of military affairs. His personal direction of the war was one of the most remarkable adminstrative achievements of this century. When the war ended, Stalin's position was unchallengeable.

But this did not mean that he had made the Soviet system palatable to the mass of the Russian people. They accepted it sullenly and in fear. An indication of this attitude was given striking proof by many thousands of Soviet citizens in Western Europe after the war—they had been brought here by the Germans—who refused to return to Russia. Some even threw themselves under trains rather than do so.

By the time Stalin died, he had become a tyrant. No one knows the precise circumstances of his death. It is probable that he died by natural causes, but the possibility that he may have been murdered cannot be excluded. I do not make this point for political purposes, but in order to enable the westerner to understand the background to Soviet thinking and to explain something of the psychology of modern Russian xenophobia, which has deeper roots than its historical predecessor. The fact is that the Russian nation has endured experiences that have no exact counterpart in the West. The national psychology has been affected, and the scars of Stalinism are printed indelibly on the minds of all who lived under Stalin's rule.

The principal economic consequence of Stalinism was the over-centralised state. In Stalin's last years, the whole nation of two hundred millions was administered from Moscow, with virtually no decentralisation. Every production unit, in the remotest part of Russia, was under direct ministerial control in Moscow—and there were several hundred ministries. As the Soviet economy developed, this system became more difficult to work. Eventually it became unworkable. As a result, Khrushchev delivered his cataclysmic denunciation of Stalin at the Twentieth Congress, in 1956.

Some of this is widely understood. But what is not so clearly appreciated is that, despite the stifling effect of much of Stalin's bureaucratic rigidity, he was responsible for much that is the basis of contemporary Russia's achievement. For example, the initial plans for investment in Soviet heavy industry and technological education as we see it today were drawn up during Stalin's last years. It was Stalin who originally set the Soviet target to outstrip the United States. It was Stalin who saw the limitations of Soviet technology in a long drawn out struggle with the West and who ordered the building of Moscow University. (The decision was taken within a few weeks of the signing of the North Atlantic Treaty Alliance in 1949, and building started that year.) And, of course, it was the 1952 Moscow Economic Conference under the aegis of Stalin that, as I have said, was the turning point in East-West trading relations. When the history of post-Stalin Russia is written, it will still bear much of Stalin's stamp.

After a brief period of rule by Malenkov, largely the representation of Stalinist bureaucracy, Khrushchev succeeded in gaining power. Whereas Malenkov drew his strength from the bureaucracy, Khrushchev controlled the Communist party *apparat*. And the conflict between these two has to be understood in these terms.

When Khrushchev decided upon his economic decentralisation, he cut away much of the power of the ministries in Moscow—a move which clearly had a political purpose as well as more practical aims. Similarly, it had been the bureaucracy he was challenging when he delivered his denunciation of Stalin the year before.

The result of these Khrushchev changes has been to produce a society that is a little more free than in Stalin's day. But it would be a mistake to try to equate it with the West—it will be two generations at least before that is possible. Contact with foreigners, however, is now possible for the Soviet citizen, although the fears and inhibitions instilled over forty years evaporate slowly. Many older people are still fearful and suspicious, but the younger generation are less inhibited. They show a genuine and overt desire for contact with the world outside the bloc; and trade can have an important effect in promoting this feeling.

From 1952 onwards, trade and other contacts became easier. At first, the change was confined largely to officially invited delegations, but after Stalin's death individual journeys from the West became an accepted pattern of communication. For their part, the Soviet Government encouraged trade and technical missions to the West. A large number of these missions placed no orders, and had no intention of doing so. In fact, they came seeking information and attempting to make up for the years of isolation. But, such increased contact is desirable and undoubtedly it has had some effect in promoting a gradual increase in the flow of trade.

This, then, is a brief background to trade between the Soviet Union and the West. The foreground follows.

2. *System of trade*

As already explained, the foreign trade of the USSR is a state monopoly under the Ministry of Foreign Trade. The broad terms of reference that are applied to Soviet Foreign Trade are intended to serve a double purpose:

1. To protect the internal economy of the Soviet Union from economic instability in the capitalist world.

2. To fulfil the import and export tasks allotted to it by the planners of the internal economy.

There is a third purpose that is likely to emerge more sharply as Soviet policies develop: the use of foreign trade as a strategic-political instrument in the new era of competitive co-existence.

It follows that the Soviet Ministry of Foreign Trade and the permanent Soviet Trade Delegations that represent it abroad are not concerned with the promotion of foreign trade, in the normal accepted sense of the term. Their task is to ensure the previously planned volume and range of imports in accordance with the requirements of the Soviet economy. Equally, they are expected to place their exports in the best market from the point of view of current Soviet political and strategic policy, which is not necessarily the most profitable market.

The actual business of export and import is conducted through the state trading organisations (see Part II, pages 165-167). These bodies have the status of juridical persons. They are responsible for arranging the terms of the trade—prices, deliveries, terms of payment— and they sign the contract. Each of these bodies is responsible for a specified range of commodities and each has its representative in the permanent Soviet Trade Delegation in the United Kingdom.*

There are no agents, either official or unofficial, of foreign firms in the Soviet Union, nor is it possible to appoint one.

Payments between the United Kingdom and the Soviet Union are normally conducted in sterling.

In the case of products that are covered by the Export of Goods (Control) Order, an export licence is required. Equally, except in the cases where products may be imported into the United Kingdom on open General Licence, or under special licensing arrangements,

* The full name and address of this organisation are: Trade Delegation of the USSR in the UK, 32, Highgate West Hill, London, N6.

which include East European countries, imports require specific import licences.*

3. *Promotion of trade and value of personal contacts*

Prospective traders should study the current Soviet economic plans and initiate enquiries with the permanent Soviet Trade Delegation in London. It is also open to them to communicate direct with the relevant import or export corporation in Moscow. But visits to Moscow should not be undertaken without thorough preparation, for they can be frustrating and disappointing unless carefully planned. All firms without previous experience in trading with the Soviet Union are recommended to consult the Commercial Relations and Exports Department of the Board of Trade which can give advice on the methods and possibilities of trading with the Soviet Union.**

Although trading with the Soviet Union means trading with a government representative, personal contacts remain of value. The human relations that it is possible to establish can be important in surmounting difficulties. Furthermore, when any new requirements of the Soviet economy are presented to the Ministry of Foreign Trade, the man or firm that is known immediately comes to mind.

Therefore serious traders must always be prepared to travel to Moscow, although such visits are the better when undertaken at the invitation of a Soviet official, who then becomes responsible for making necessary appointments.

It is particularly important that any business visitor to Russia should inform the British Embassy in Moscow of his intended trip and should call at the Embassy when he arrives.***

4. *Travel facilities*

Travel facilities to Russia are now almost the same as those to any other country. An excellent air service is in operation. It is also possible to go by train or ship, and any travel agent will make the necessary arrangements.

* Detailed information will be supplied by Board of Trade (Export Licensing Branch), Atlantic House, Holborn Viaduct, London, EC1. (Tel. City 5733).

** Board of Trade (Commercial Relations and Exports Department), Horse Guards Avenue, London, SW1. (Tel. Trafalgar 8855).

*** Its address is: British Embassy, Sofiiskaya Naberezhnaya No. 14, Moscow. (Tel. VI 95-55).

The main difference between a journey to Moscow and to any western capital is that the hotel arrangements in Russia are handled by the Soviet travel agency *Intourist*. This organisation assumes omnipotent responsibility for the western visitor on arrival. An *Intourist* car awaits him at the airport. The hotels reserved for foreigners are under the control of *Intourist*. The same body also provides an interpreter, when required, who fulfils the functions of a guide as well. Most of the interpreters are trained by the foreign languages institutions in Russia and prove to be ardent partisans of the Communist philosophy: therefore political argument with them is not a rewarding pastime for western visitors.

One aspect of *Intourist* procedure requires explanation. The western visitor needs to equip himself with travel vouchers before he leaves Britain. These travel voucher books, obtainable through the London agents of *Intourist*, cover the cost of his hotel, meals and the use of a car; and the appropriate coupons have to be detached from time to time. In short, they supply the substitute for a form of travellers' cheque, although it is possible to cash a recognised travellers' cheque in a Soviet Bank in Moscow in the normal way. However, outside Moscow, in the more remote towns, the main British banks are still unknown, and it is usually wise not to leave Moscow without adequate supplies of Soviet currency.

5. Seven Year Plan

The Soviet Economic Plan, 1959-1965, must be studied in detail because all trade has to be conducted within its framework. The basic aim of the plan is to raise Soviet industrial output to the same level as that of the United States of America, but at the present rate of progress it is questionable whether this can be achieved until several years later.

The 1965 target is to produce 65-70 million tons of pig iron, up to 86-91 million tons of steel and 65-70 million tons of rolled stock. Most of the developments will be large expansions of existing plants.

A much more rapid development of the chemical industry is also intended to take advantage of the country's natural resources and to make it a major source for raw materials for consumer goods.

The plan foreshadows a change in the pattern of fuel production by concentrating on the development of more economic fuels such as oil and natural gas, instead of coal.

Other major aims of the Seven Year Plan are:

1. rapid development of electrification of all branches of the economy by building, chiefly, large scale power plants;

2. the technical reconstruction of the railways on the basis of electrification and the wider use of diesel locomotives;

3. a major housing drive aimed at eliminating the chronic housing shortage that has been a feature of Soviet society.

The Plan also envisages much greater uses of natural resources beginning with land. The Virgin Lands drive is already a part of the main attempt to increase agricultural production, which is the worst feature of the Communist production system and a heavy indictment of the Marxist-Leninist doctrine of collective farming. It is intended to build a powerful new metallurgical centre on the basis of the iron ore deposits newly discovered in Siberia and Kazakhstan.* Simultaneously the non-ferrous metals industry in Kazakhstan, Central Asia, the Urals and the Baikal region will be expanded. The power industry in Siberia is to be developed on the basis of cheap coal from the new minefields, as also will be the oil industry in the Caucasus and the Ukraine. Finally, the authorities intend to exploit the plentiful supplies of timber that will become available as Siberia is developed.

The prospect offered by the Seven Year Plan is immense capital investment—almost double that of the previous seven years—and it is here that the main opportunities for western trade lie. But, lest there is undue optimism, it is clearly stated in the plan that the Soviet Union's trade with the other countries of the bloc is to increase by more than 50 per cent by the end of 1965.

As the second priority, the plan envisages increased trade with the under-developed countries; and only third place is given to the capitalist areas of the world. The liberalisation that has taken place since the assumption of power by Khrushchev does not go further than that.

6. *Anglo-Soviet Trade Treaty*

The Eccles Mission to Moscow, May 1959, negotiated a Five Year Trade Agreement in which the Soviet Government provided a list of

* For map showing the location of the principal new projects in the Eastern Regions of the USSR see the Soviet Journal *Voprosy Ekonomiki* (American translation), Vol. II, Number 5, September 1959.

machinery and equipment 'for possible import' from the United Kingdom in the period 1960-1964. The value placed by the Soviet authorities on the listed equipment was approximately 4 to 4.5 billion roubles (£350-£400 millions at the official rate of exchange). In addition the Soviet delegation could also purchase in the United Kingdom during the same period industrial goods and raw materials to the approximate value of 3 to 3.5 billion roubles (£276-£300 million at the official rate of exchange) including, chemicals, pipes for gas pipe lines, and rolled ferrous metals, as well as raw materials traditionally purchased.

The text of the Anglo-Soviet Trade Treaty and the list of 'possible purchases' are added below.

FIVE YEAR TRADE AGREEMENT between the United Kingdom of Great Britain and Northern Ireland and the Union of Soviet Socialist Republics.

The Government of the United Kingdom of Great Britain and Northern Ireland and the Government of the Union of Soviet Socialist Republics,

having taken note of the benefits to both countries which arise from trade between the United Kingdom and the Soviet Union,

believing that the further development of this trade is in the mutual interest of both countries,

desiring to create a firmer foundation for the development of Anglo-Soviet trade,

have agreed as follows:

ARTICLE 1

(1) The United Kingdom Government and the Government of the Soviet Union look forward to a steady increase in trade between the two countries over the period of this Agreement both in goods which have traditionally been exchanged between them and in new ones.

(2) To this end both Governments will, within the scope of the laws and regulations in force in their respective countries, facilitate the exchange of goods and services between the two countries on a mutually advantageous basis, without prejudice to the right of either Government to refrain from taking any measures under the present Agreement inconsistent with their essential security interests.

ARTICLE 2

(1) The United Kingdom Government expect that, beginning in the first year of the present Agreement, there will be a substantial increase in the total volume of the imports, under normal commercial conditions, of traditional goods from the Soviet Union into the United Kingdom under

Open General Import Licence, including grain, timber and timber products, wood pulp, manganese ore, asbestos, ferro-alloys, non-ferrous metals, mineral fertilisers, flax and other goods.

(2) The United Kingdom Government and the Government of the Soviet Union will arrange, in cases of necessity, for the Board of Trade in the United Kingdom and the Trade Delegation of the USSR in the United Kingdom respectively to establish by mutual agreement, and in a spirit of friendly understanding, quotas on an appropriate basis for the import into the United Kingdom of any Soviet goods not subject to Open General Import Licence, and not otherwise provided for in the present Agreement.

ARTICLE 3

The Government of the Soviet Union expect that the Soviet Foreign Trade Organisations will place, on normal commercial conditions and having regard to Article 2, substantial orders in the United Kingdom for equipment for the manufacture of synthetic fibres, synthetic materials and manufactures from them, and also other types of equipment for the chemical industry; equipment for the pulp and paper industry; forging, stamping and casting equipment; metal-working machine tools; equipment for the electro-technical and cable industry; equipment and instruments for the automation of production processes; pumping, compression and refrigeration equipment; equipment for sugar beet factories and other types of equipment for the food industry; equipment for the building industry, light industry and other branches of industry as well as industrial products and raw materials customarily bought from United Kingdom firms.

ARTICLE 4

(1) Both Governments will facilitate an increase in the exchange of consumer goods between the United Kingdom and the Soviet Union. It is understood that the facilities to be granted for the exchange of consumer goods by one party will be approximately of the same value as the facilities to be granted by the other party.

(2) The lists of consumer goods which are to be the subject of such exchanges during the period from the 1st of July, 1959, to the 30th of June, 1960, and during the subsequent annual periods will be agreed from year to year between the competent United Kingdom authorities and the Trade Delegation of the USSR in the United Kingdom.

(3) Negotiations on the lists for the first year shall take place within six weeks of the signing of the present Agreement. It is contemplated that for that period additional facilities each way to the value of approximately £2 million will be granted over and above the value of the consumer goods which were exchanged between the two countries in 1958.

(4) The lists of goods for exchange will, for example, include:

United Kingdom goods: motor vehicles, textile manufactures, including cotton textiles, ready-made clothing, knitwear and hosiery;

footwear; floor coverings; carpets (machine made); leather goods; medicines; photographic materials; sports goods; musical instruments; toys; cured herrings and white fish; and

Soviet goods: motor cars; cameras; watches; matches; musical instruments; carpets (hand knotted); medicines; toys; handicrafts; tinned crab; vodka; wines and brandies.

ARTICLE 5

Representatives of the two Governments will meet once a year (or more frequently on the proposal of one of them) to examine the carrying out of the provisions of the present Agreement and if necessary to prepare recommendations to one or both of the Governments for the further improvement of trade relations between the two countries. The meetings of representatives referred to in this Article will normally take place alternately in London and Moscow.

ARTICLE 6

The United Kingdom Government and the Government of the Soviet Union agree to continue to allow the ships of both countries to participate in the trade between the two countries and to follow the principle of free and fair competition in international shipping.

ARTICLE 7

The United Kingdom Government and the Government of the Soviet Union will permit their organisations or business concerns to make available industrial and technical information to organisations or business concerns in the other country subject to the relevant legal and administrative requirements of the country providing this information and in accordance with normal commercial practice.

ARTICLE 8

In the first half of 1960 both Governments will enter into negotiations for the conclusion of a Treaty of Commerce and Navigation between the United Kingdom and the Soviet Union, which will replace the Temporary Trade Agreement between the two countries of the 16th of February, 1934.

ARTICLE 9

The present Agreement shall come into force on the date of signature and shall remain in force until the 30th of June, 1964.

In witness whereof the undersigned, duly authorised to that effect, have signed the present Agreement.

Done in Moscow, the 24th of May, 1959, in duplicate, both in the English and Russian languages, and both texts being equally authentic.

For the Government of the United Kingdom of Great Britain and Northern Ireland.	For the Government of the Union of Soviet Socialist Republics
DAVID ECCLES	N. PATOLICHEV

List of equipment for possible import from the United Kingdom to the USSR in 1960-1964.

1. Equipment of a Factory for production of polyacrylinitril fibre and semi-products, capacity 15,000 tons annually   1 unit
2. Equipment of a Factory for production of high tenacity rayon tire cord fibre, capacity 50 tons daily (24 hours)   1 ,,
3. Equipment of a Factory for production of 'AH' salt   1 ,,
4. Equipment of a Factory for production of helium from natural gases   1 ,,
5. Equipment of Factories for chemical treatment of germanium   2 ,,
6. Equipment for continuous polymerization of caprolactam, capacity 12 tons daily (24 hours)   1 ,,
7. Equipment for recovery and regeneration of carbon disulphide, capacity 70 tons daily (24 hours)   1 ,,
8. Plant for production of polyester resins for glass plastics capacity 5,000 tons annually   1 ,,
9. Equipment of a Factory for production of copolymers of styrene, capacity 5,000 tons annually   1 ,,
10. Equipment of a Factory for production of tripolyphosphate 1 ,,
11. Equipment of a Factory for production of porophors   1 ,,
12. Equipment of a Factory for production of acetate silk, capacity 5,100 tons annually   1 ,,
13. Equipment of a Factory for production of activated black from liquid raw materials   1 ,,
14. Equipment for production of articles from synthetic materials (polyethylene, polychlorvinyl, etc.)   100 million roubles
15. Equipment for production of fat synthetic alcohols, capacity 5,000 tons annually   2 units
16. Equipment for production of alkylamides of synthetic fat acids, capacity 5,000 tons annually   1 ,,
17. Spinning, weaving and finishing equipment for production of articles of synthetic fibres   80-100 million roubles
18. Twisting machines for production of 'Elastic' fibre   150 pieces
19. Equipment of a factory for production of styrene and shock resistant polystyrene, capacity 20,000 tons annually   1 unit
20. Equipment for continuous production of phenolformaldehyde resins, capacity 30,000 tons annually   1 ,,
21. Equipment of a Factory for production of glass plastic plates together with resins, capacity 20,000 tons annually   1 ,,
22. Equipment of a Factory for production of 'AH' salt and '66' nylon, capacity 10,000 tons of nylon annually   1 ,,
23. Equipment of a Factory for production of acetate staple, capacity 20,000 tons annually   1 ,,
24. Equipment for production of polychlorvinyl resin, capacity 35,000-40.000 tons annually   1 ,,

25. Equipment of a Factory for production of plastic and glass-plastic pipes, capacity 20,000 tons annually   1 unit

26. Equipment of a Factory for production of styrpore, capacity 10,000 tons annually   1 „

27. Equipment for production of tetrafluorethylene, capacity 3,000 tons annually   1 „

28. Equipment of a Factory for production of synthetic glycerine, capacity 20,000 tons annually   1 „

29. Equipment of a Factory for production of ethylene urea, capacity 1,000 tons annually   1 „

30. Miscellaneous chemical equipment   100 million roubles

31. Equipment of cellulose works and board making equipment   200-220 million roubles

32. Paper making machines for production of newsprint, capacity 340 tons daily (24 hours)   2 units

33. Equipment of sugar Works for treatment of 5,000 tons sugar beet daily (24 hours) each   15 „

34. Equipment for complex automation of ore dressing and coal dressing factories   40-50 million roubles

35. Rolling mills equipment, including multi-high mills for cold rolling of ferrous and non-ferrous strips up to .05 mm. thick and up to 1500 mm. wide   15-20 million roubles

36. Casting equipment, including multi-station forming automatic machines, shell moulding machines, hydro-electric flaskless moulding machines, automatic core multi-station blowing machines, universal sand blowing core makers   30-40 million roubles

37. Forging equipment and presses, including transfer machines   60-70 million roubles

38. Machine tools, including special multiple head machines, with programme control, gear tooth cutting and grinding machines, internal grinding machines with heads operating at the speeds of 100,000-120,000 revolutions per minute, planetary spindle grinding machines and automatic machines for machining turbine and compressor blades   100-120 million roubles

39. Automatic transfer machine tools   350-400 million roubles

40. Equipment for production of small size bearings including electronic machines for size control and sorting balls, rollers, and other parts   3 Units

41. Machines for cutting, grinding and polishing thin-walled pipes of various diameters   15-20 million roubles

42. Electrical equipment   80-100 million roubles

J

43. Equipment for cable industry, including insulating machines, cable twisting and insulation coating machines, machines for production of co-axial electric cables — 80-100 million roubles

44. Equipment for production of electro-vacuum articles and transistor instruments — 15 million roubles

45. Radio-television, control and measuring instruments, telecommunication apparatus and instruments for automation of technological processes, including quantometers, electronic and high frequency radio measuring instruments — 90-100 million roubles

46. Pumps and compressors, including pumps for operation with aggressive media, vacuum pumps and multi-stage compressors of various capacities — 90-100 million roubles

47. Refrigerating equipment, including deep freezing plants and conditioners for industrial use — 90-100 million roubles

48. Valves of large parameters and acid proof valves complete with automatic control system — 40-50 million roubles

49. Equipment for food industry — 300-320 million roubles

50. Equipment for construction industry — 50-60 million roubles

51. Equipment for polygraphical industry — 50-60 million roubles

52. Equipment for light industry — 120-150 million roubles

53. Other equipment for various industries — 250-300 million roubles

The text of the Anglo-Soviet trade agreement and the list of equipment are reproduced with acknowledgements to the *Board of Trade Journal*.

CHAPTER III

The East European Countries

1. *General*

The East European countries of the Communist bloc form an economic pattern within the general framework of *Comecon*. As with foreign policy, the main economic policy is determined by the Soviet Union—but with certain margins of self-determination permitted to each individual country.

The background to the economies of the East European countries lies in their post-war political history. Their Communist governments were nearly all superimposed on unwilling peoples in the aftermath of war. The detailed history of the Communist take-overs varies in each case but the pattern is broadly the same.

In the immediate post-war months, nearly all these countries had begun their peacetime regimes with coalition governments that included Communists. (In France, too, the Government had included Communists—something that it is difficult to envisage now.) But in the second stage, in Eastern Europe, the non-Communists in the Coalition governments were removed; their places were taken by Communist sympathisers, and many of the previous non-Communist ministers were put on trial, or—like Micolajczyk, the Polish Premier —fled to the West. Then followed a third stage in the East European development, when the Communists took over completely.

This last stage in the process of effecting Communist control was partly accelerated by the Marshall Plan in 1947. The immediate reaction to the Plan of some of the East European countries had been favourable. Czechoslovakia, in particular, saw merit in it and she still had a coalition government at the time. In other East European countries, there were also indications of a desire to take part in the

Marshall Aid schemes. But the Soviet Union took up a completely different position.

After agreeing to attend the first Marshall Plan conference in Paris, the Soviet Delegation withdrew, denouncing the plan as 'dollar diplomacy'. Pressure was brought to bear on the East European countries to follow suit. They did. And where there was any opposition among them, to the Moscow policy, it was eliminated as quickly as possible.

The Soviet Government's attitude to the Marshall Plan was motivated by the belief that such a scheme would loosen the ties in eastern Europe and would lead eventually to the breaking of the Communist grip. The Soviet response therefore, was to bind those ties yet closer and out of this new situation came *Comecon*.

As already explained (see pages 108-111), the basic object of *Comecon* was to bring about the eventual integration and the self-sufficiency of the bloc. In theory, each country was allotted specific economic and industrial functions within the bloc. Raw material sources in some countries were supposed to be tied to industrial production in others. Rationalisation of industrial production was also agreed in theory.

But *Comecon* proved ineffective during the last years of Stalin for two reasons. First, the industrial chauvinism that had become the characteristic of the Soviet Union at the time was also made the feature of economic planning in most of the East European countries. In short, Stalinist Russia was the model and the object of each local Communist Government was to copy it down to the last detail. Thus, every country set out to duplicate what was already happening in Russia, and the theory of *Comecon* consequently went by the board.

The second reason for the failure of *Comecon* was that no effective administrative machinery was established to implement its theoretical purpose. During Stalin's lifetime—and for some years after his death —no more than lip service was paid to *Comecon's* declared purpose. It was only with the advent of Khrushchev that *Comecon* began to assume its current reality.

It is still too early to forecast the ultimate consequences of *Comecon* but the long-term pattern is beginning to emerge. Each country will manufacture certain products; but for others it will be dependent on the members of the Soviet bloc. In some cases they will be dependent on them for manufactured products, in others for raw materials.

The most striking example of this economic inter-dependence within the bloc is the new Soviet oil pipeline, now in the process of construction. Under the scheme, the East European countries will all receive piped crude oil from the Soviet Union, thereby providing plentiful fuel supplies for industrial expansion. The responsibility for the building of the pipelines rests on the governments of each of the East European countries through which they pass. But there is to be a pooling of resources and technical information within the bloc to facilitate the vast project.

The aim of the oil pipeline network is clearly economic. But a study of the map shows that the scheme is also drawn up with an eye to political considerations. For instance, the pipeline runs for a long way through Czechoslovakia—a safe political risk for the Communist point of view—before turning south sharply into Hungary.

As with the Soviet Union, the declared aim of the East European countries is to bring about the economic self-sufficiency of the Communist bloc. However, in some of the East European countries the part played by trade with countries outside the bloc makes them partly dependent on outside markets and sources of supply. This is particularly true of Poland, Czechoslovakia and East Germany. To a lesser extent, Hungary also has traditional foreign trade relations with the non-Communist world.

2. Poland

From the trade point of view, Poland is the most important of the East European countries. She has the largest population, but she also depends heavily on the non-Communist countries for markets for her agricultural produce. No assessment of Poland's economy, however brief, is accurate without reference to the devastation she suffered during the war. A fifth of her population—six to seven million people—perished. Her loss of capital and buildings ranged from a quarter to a fifth of the pre-war stock. Warsaw, itself, was largely destroyed. In the 1939-45 war Poland suffered greater losses proportionately to her size and wealth than any other country.

On top of this, a large part of pre-war Poland was annexed by the

Soviet Union, and in compensation Poland received the former German territories as far west as the Rivers Oder and Neisse. Several million people were ejected from their homes in the new Soviet territories and driven west to the former German lands, where, in their turn, several million Germans had been driven out and also sent further west.

The westward shift created a more compact Poland, with better communications and a wide access to the sea, including the ports of Gdansk (formerly Danzig) and Szczecin (Stettin). The Upper Silesian coalfield became entirely Polish, and it was augmented by high quality coking coal in the Walbrzych basin in Lower Silesia. Rich brown coal deposits, a highly developed communications system in Silesia, and access to the River Oder also fell to Poland. The agricultural land in the new territories, although less in area than the parts ceded to the Soviet Union, was on the whole of better quality.

Broadly, the circumstances were created for a viable Polish economy, if it had not been for the mistakes of the country's Communist leadership and exploitation by the Soviet Union before 1956. As I have already indicated, the period while Stalin was still alive was characterised by excessive duplication in the East European countries of the Soviet programme for industrialisation—and Poland was a case in point.

The first five years after the war were taken up with national reconstruction and assimilation of Poland's new frontiers. With the help of $500 million worth of help from UNNRA, Poland's overall industrial production recovered its pre-war level. But the *per capita* supplies of food and consumer goods remained below the 1939 figure. The natural tendency at that point therefore, might have been to concentrate the main efforts in the next period of the Six Year Plan (1950-1955) on the section of the national economy that was still lagging. In the event, the decision taken by the Polish Communist Government was the reverse. Industrialisation was intensified. Agriculture and the consumer goods industries were largely set on one side.

Symbolic of this policy was the 'Lenin Metallurgical Combine' at Nowa Huta. This large plant, started in 1950 at great expense, aimed at doubling Poland's steel production. It is symbolic in its neglect of the workers, so vividly described in Adam Wazyk's *Poem for*

Adults—with the workers living in bad conditions in shoddy and fantastically ill-designed tenements. It is also symbolic in its siting, which was political, not economic: Nowa Huta was 50 miles from the Silesian coalfields from which the plant must draw its fuel. On the other hand, it is adjacent to Cracow, the ancient capital of the Polish kings and the centre of Polish tradition.

At the end of the Six Year Plan, Poland's industrial output had more than doubled, but the supply of food was only slightly larger than in 1950. The main instrument of the Government's agricultural policy was the state farm, rather than the collective. This was because the Polish peasantry who were in the vast majority, remained obstinate and unwilling to join in any collectivisation programmes. Thus the Government's policy of discriminating against the private farmer had the overall effect of retarding food production. By 1955 Poland, a pre-war net exporter of food, had become instead a net importer.

The housing position had also become critical. The supply of new accommodation had not kept pace with the population increase, and in the rural areas the situation was particularly bad. Meanwhile existing accommodation for 600,000 people had fallen into an advanced state of dilapidation.

Not least because of the Polish Government's Stalinist policies, real wages in 1955 were at the same level as in 1949.

It was this combination of economic misery, allied to the loosening of political restraints, that led to the Poznan riots in June 1956 and the change in the Polish leadership in October of the same year. The new leader, Wladyslaw Gomulka, who had been imprisoned as a Titoist, was brought back in the face of bitter Soviet opposition. His immediate task was to avert national bankruptcy. At first, his main success was in agriculture. The removal of many of the discriminations against the private farmer coupled with the virtual collapse of the collectivisation programme led to an outstanding harvest in 1957. In industry, where he departed less from the orthodox dogma of Communism, Gomulka was only partly successful. Inflationary pressures and a large trade deficit developed. The situation was saved by credits from the Soviet Union worth $400 million and by an American loan of nearly $100 million.

The following year, 1958, was a good one in which the main targets for the economic plan were achieved. Gradually people became better clad and there were more goods in the shops. Thus, in 1958, industrial production went up by over 9 per cent and agricultural production by over 3 per cent.

The current Seven Year Plan (1959-1965) envisages similar annual increases in industrial production, so that if the plan is successfully achieved by 1965, the total increase over 1959 should be 80 per cent. The Plan appears to be realistic, but as the emphasis is still on capital investment, there are not likely to be any sharp increases in living standards for a long time to come.

In agriculture, whereas collectivisation remains the declared aim, greater faith is being placed in the loose associations called 'Agricultural Circles'. These are a form of producer co-operation by which the Government hopes to persuade the peasantry of the value of co-operative methods. A major plan for investment in farm mechanisation, also, is canalised through the 'Agricultural Circles'.

Poland's foreign trade is less concentrated on the bloc than any other East European country. Even so, the bloc absorbs about 75 per cent of Polish exports of machinery and equipment, whereas the non-Communist countries take the major proportion of the exports of foodstuffs, textiles and coal. Thus a problem of export expansion to the West faces Poland, if she wishes to increase imports from non-Communist sources.

The Seven Year Plan envisages a rather slower growth of trade than of output. It is expected for example, that the total trade turnover will rise by 46 per cent whereas the net domestic product will probably go up by 60 per cent and industrial production by over 80 per cent. The plan provides for increasing concentration on manufactured goods for export, especially equipment, and there must be big increases in imports of raw materials.

3. Czechoslovakia

Czechoslovakia, which used to be referred to as 'the model democracy', became Communist after the *coup d'etat* of 1948. It had been carved out of the old Austro-Hungarian Empire, together with a small part of Imperial Germany. Under Thomas Masaryk, its founder, Czechoslovakia developed into a parliamentary democracy with civil liberties broadly on the same lines as those of western Europe. To that extent she was unique amongst the East European countries. She was also the most advanced industrially, and the pre-war Czechoslovak economy, particularly in foreign trade, was closely linked with the West.

The turning point in the political alignment of Czechoslovakia was the Munich Agreement. From that moment onwards, there was a gradual loosening of the ties with the western democracies and a growing tendency to look more and more towards Moscow as the predominant influence in Czech external economic policies. In the circumstances that followed the Second World War, this growing Russian influence was given a further impetus by the fact that it was the Russian military forces that liberated Prague—the nearby American troops deliberately holding back on instructions from above.

After liberation, the Republic was restored under President Benes. It had a coalition government at first, including Communists. Six months later, in December 1945, all Soviet and American forces were withdrawn. In the first and only free elections, held in early 1946, the Communists polled nearly 40 per cent of the votes and Gottwald, the Czech Communist Party Leader, became Prime Minister in another coalition government, but more left than its predecessor.

The next important development was the offer of Marshall Aid a year later which, as already stated, was accepted unanimously by the Czechoslovak Government—only for the decision to be reversed following representations from the Soviet Union. It was clear by now that it was the intention of the Gottwald Government to throw in Czechoslovakia's lot with the Soviet bloc; and in the following year the Czech Communists effected the *coup d'etat* that eliminated all pretence of the continuing coalition. This *coup* was one of main events that awakened the West to the perils of the growing Cold War. It led directly to the Western Union Treaty and, later, to the North Atlantic Treaty Alliance.

The Czech Communists thus succeeded to the political control of a small but highly industrialised country which had suffered much less in the war than Poland. Since then, the Communist hold on the country has never been relaxed in the same way as that on some of the other East European countries. For example, the easements that followed Khrushchev's denunciation of Stalin in 1956 found little place in Czechoslovakia. Equally, the political turbulence in 1956 that afflicted her neighbours, Poland and Hungary, also had no counterpart in Czechoslovakia. Therefore she is regarded as amongst the most 'loyal' of the countries of the Soviet bloc.

Before the war, over 80 per cent of Czechoslovakia's foreign trade was with the West. Now, over 75 per cent is with the Soviet bloc. This gives a striking indication of the redeployment of external economic policy and it shows the extent to which the internal Czech economy is now related to the policies of the bloc, within the framework of *Comecon*.

The closer economic alignment with the East was shown first by the abrupt curtailment of foreign trade after 1948. Instead, it was diverted eastward. As a result there had to be a substantial increase in Czechoslovak heavy industry to meet the Soviet bloc's demand for more capital goods. Considerable expansions in heavy industry plants and new towns were ordered. Much of it was concentrated in Slovakia, previously a backward rural area.

This trend towards heavy industry continues and by 1965 it is envisaged that industrial production will rise by a further 90 per cent, whereas personal consumption is to increase by only 45 per cent.

The industrial growth of the country has not been matched by improvements in agriculture. Under the Second Five Year Plan (1956-1960) gross agricultural production was to increase at an approximate average of 6 per cent per year; but, in fact, the total increase in the first three years amounted to six per cent. Collectivisation has been stepped up during the same period, and to this policy must be ascribed the main reason for the slow progress. A striking illustration of the practical effect of collectivisation was given by the Czech Minister of Finance in February 1959. He said that whilst there were 73 pigs per 100 hectares on collective farms, there were 417 per 100 hectares on the small private plots permitted to collective farmers.

To summarise: Czechoslovakia's manufacturing industry is so important to the bloc that her present emphasis on trade with it is not likely to change, although in the economic competition that is likely to develop in underdeveloped countries the Czech economy is certain to play an increasing part as a political instrument of Soviet bloc policy. There are already indications of this trend, as witness greater Czech interest in Middle Eastern and Latin American markets, and more examples are likely to follow.

4. *Hungary*

The Hungary of today is largely the country whose frontiers were delineated by the Treaty of Trianon, signed in 1920. Before the Second World War, except for a brief period of Communist government under Bela Kun in 1919, successive Hungarian governments were politically of the extreme right wing or neo-fascist. During this period, Hungary's main aim in foreign policy was to regain 'the lost territories' that she had been compelled to cede under the Treaty of Trianon and which had formed part of the Austro-Hungarian Empire. On the other hand, Poland, Czechoslovakia, Roumania and Jugoslavia had a vested interest in resisting this policy.

From 1938 onwards, Admiral Horthy, the so-called Regent of Hungary, exploited the situation in Eastern Europe following Munich to further this thwarted aim. For a brief period he succeeded in regaining some of these territories under 'The Vienna Awards', granted by Hitler in wartime.

The consequence of the defeat of Hitler was to return Hungary's frontiers to the Trianon lines under the Peace Treaty signed in 1947.

Like Poland and Czechoslovakia, Hungary began the post-war period with a coalition government which included Communists. Progressively the non-Communists were removed. Some were imprisoned and others were deported to the Soviet Union. By mid-1947, the Communist grip was complete; and from then onwards Hungary became a member of the Soviet bloc, and joined the Cominform. Thus the Marshall Plan never reached the stage of formal acceptance—as with the Czechs.

Despite the 1947 Peace Treaty, Hungary was never free of Soviet troops because they were allowed to remain indefinitely for communication purposes pending agreement on the Austrian Treaty, which was not signed until 1955. And then, in 1956, there was the Hungarian uprising. This stemmed, as did the events in Poland, from the de-Stalinisation that followed the Khrushchev speech to the Twentieth Congress. First, the Stalinist dictator of Hungary, Rakosi, was replaced by his shadow, Gerö. Janos Kadar, who like Gomulka, had been imprisoned as a 'Titoist' was brought back into the Government in an attempt to assuage public opinion. This proved insufficient.

The revolution was touched off on 23rd October, 1956 by student demonstrations. One of the students' demands was that Nagy, who had been Prime Minister for a short period following Stalin's death (during which he is reported to have released 93,000 political prisoners) should become the head of the Government again. Rioting and shooting continued for over a week. Most of the Hungarian Army and police sided with the demonstrators. More and more concessions were won from the Communist leaders. Eventually Nagy became Prime Minister, Gerö was replaced by Kadar as First Secretary of the Communist Party; and the Soviet forces, which had borne the brunt of the fighting, withdrew from Budapest.

A coalition government was formed of 'National Communists', Smallholders, Social Democrats and Peasants. With amazing rapidity the visible trappings of Stalinism, such as street names and the huge statue of Stalin in the capital, disappeared. Trade unions and workers' councils were reconstituted and suppressed newspapers reappeared.

Under great public pressure, Nagy declared Hungary to be a neutral state, withdrew from the Warsaw Pact and appealed to the United Nations for support. This proved too much for the Soviet Government, whose troops were ordered back into Budapest. Bitter fighting followed, which lasted nearly a fortnight before the Russian authorities achieved control. Kadar, who defected from the Nagy Government, was installed as the head of the puppet Hungarian Communist Government. Nagy himself was arrested by the Soviet authorities, after he left the Jugoslav Embassy on a safe conduct pass issued by Kadar, and was executed 18 months later.

The cost of the revolution to Hungary was very considerable. The Kadar regime admitted 2,700 killed and over 20,000 wounded. It is believed that a further 30,000 were deported to Russia, where many remain. Nearly 200,000 people of all ages fled to the West. The suppression of the revolution was followed by weeks of industrial disaffection. Industrial production dropped considerably and the food position became critical. The Soviet Government thereupon formulated a new policy towards Hungary, involving slight political easements, the granting of credits and the release of more consumer goods.

The result of the new policy has been a gradual stabilisation of the position. The Kadar regime is now more firmly entrenched than before, but it does not enjoy popular support as yet. Rather, it has the resigned acceptance of a large section of the population who believe that there is no practical alternative.

In this politically turbulent situation, industrial development has been spasmodic. Before the Second World War, the share of industry in the national income (35 per cent) was only marginally above that of agriculture (34 per cent). By 1958, industry's share was claimed to be 46 per cent as against agriculture's 33 per cent. During the period of Communist rule, industrial expansion has fluctuated. For instance, in 1951 it rose 30 per cent. In 1954 it increased 3 per cent. In 1956, the year of the revolution, it fell 9 per cent. Only in 1959 did it return to its pre-revolution level, but now it is advancing gradually.

The First Five Year Plan (1950-1954) led to excessive concentration on heavy industry—as in nearly all the major East European countries. For example, the investment in the Stalin Steel Plant alone exceeded all the investments in light industry. This posed serious problems for the economy, especially as Hungary is particularly short of the raw materials and fuel necessary for the industrial sector. The Second Five Year Plan, which was abandoned after the revolution, proceeded along similar, if slightly less ambitious, lines. In 1957, a new and more realistic Three Year Plan was substituted.

As with Czechoslovakia, Hungary's foreign trade has been reorientated since she joined the Soviet bloc. In 1938, only 10 per cent of Hungary's foreign trade was with the countries that now make up the bloc. Now it is over 67 per cent, and it is intended that this figure will rise to 75 per cent by 1965.

Most of the credits granted by the Soviet Union have been in the form of raw materials. Repayment is to be made mainly by Hungarian exports to Russia—all of which adds to the process by which Hungary's foreign trade leans towards the Communist bloc.

In the face of this concentration on industrial production, it is not surprising that progress in agriculture has not kept pace, although in the richness of her soil Hungary resembles Denmark. Collectivisation made spasmodic progress until 1956, when there was a general exodus from the co-operatives. However, the Kadar Government has reasserted the Communist policy gradually, and in 1958 a new drive was launched. By 1959, nearly a third of the land had again been collectivised and there are signs that this tempo will be increased.

The pattern of Hungary's economy falls therefore into the general pattern of eastern Europe, with the additional circumstances that politically and economically the Government is even more dependent upon the Soviet Union than are Czechoslovakia and Poland, and her opportunities for foreign trade outside the bloc are accordingly limited.

5. *Eastern Germany*

The East German Republic (DDR) has been fashioned out of the former Soviet military zone of occupation. Its origins and *raison d'etre* are to be found in the fundamental disagreements of the Cold War.

The conflict over Germany was first made clear by the different attitudes towards reparations, as shown by the Soviet Union and the western powers. Whereas the former was primarily concerned with making good the ravages and devastation caused to Russia by the German invasion, the western powers' immediate post-war policy was to see that the economy of vanquished Germany did not become a major liability to the occupying powers.

Because of this initial difference, no German Peace Treaty was possible. And when the western powers introduced currency reforms in early 1948—as a shock treatment to the West Germany economy —the divisions over Germany hardened yet further. The Soviet answer at the time was to blockade the land approaches to western Berlin, where the western allies retained occupation rights under the instrument of German surrender signed in May 1945. The western powers retorted with the Berlin airlift. At that point the Cold War nearly became a hot war. Eventually the Berlin blockade was lifted, but during the period of the airlift the Iron Curtain across Germany became a reality.

The practical effect of the division of Germany was to create, side by side, two separate German states with two different economic systems. Whereas West Germany became a classic free enterprise society, the Soviet occupation gradually created an orthodox communist state in the East zone.

In the period immediately following the war's end, the Russian policy was to dismantle German industrial installations and remove them to the Soviet Union. After a short time, this policy changed.

The dismantling was stopped. Instead, the major factories in the East zone were placed under direct Russian control. Raw materials were made available by Russian orders; and, instead of capital machinery, the products of the factories were sent back to the Soviet Union as reparations. Under the Russian control another change was brought about in the East German industries—key positions in each organisation were gradually filled by German Communists working under Soviet orders, the former executives being 'transferred' or fleeing to the West. In this way the apparatus of the East German Communist State was established.

Life was extremely hard in East Germany throughout the early post-war period. Shortages were acute. Political persecution was widespread. The result was a constant stream of refugees to the West, the main and easiest point of escape being Berlin itself. Eventually the East German conditions became so bad that major demonstrations broke out on 17th June, 1953. Order was restored by Soviet military forces.

After this event there was a gradual but marked easement in conditions in East Germany—as in the case of Hungary. Norms were reduced. More food and consumer goods were made available. Greater contact with the West was permitted. In the new circumstances East Germany became more and more the *entrepreneur* of East-West trade, with East Berlin its centre. Eventually this period ended, too, and the countries of the Soviet bloc came to deal with the West more directly. Thus, in the conditions prevailing today the trading importance of East Germany has declined once more to the point decided by its own foreign trade needs rather than by its role as a trading go-between.

East Germany has brought new technologies and precision skills to the economy of the Soviet bloc. For this reason, her trade eastwards expanded rapidly. As I have said, this trade was first in the form of reparations; but after the 1953 easements and the eventual granting of sovereignty to East Germany, it has taken on the normal form. The role given East Germany by *Comecon* has regularised the position. Her trade westwards has been conducted largely through West Germany. This has been so partly for political reasons, to keep alive the issue of German re-unification; but it has also a more practical basis. Many enterprises in West Germany retained ties with people in the East zone, and, despite communisation, some of the original business relationships remained. Language and race further cemented these ties to the point that some British companies now do business with East Germany through West German agents.

6. Bulgaria, Roumania, Albania

These three countries form a separate category within the bloc. Their economies are largely backward and rural, and their dependence on the Soviet Union is complete.

The Communist period in Bulgaria has been marked, as in the case of all the East European countries, with the drive for industrialisation. This has been carried on despite the lack of a suitable basis of raw materials for heavy industry. The position now is that Bulgaria has developed a small amount of heavy industry at great expense. But, for her raw materials, she is dependent upon the Soviet Union. For this reason, nearly all her foreign trade is with Russia, although actual statistics—as with Roumania and Albania—are unobtainable.

Under the Bulgarian Third Five Year Plan (1958-1962), heavy industry continues to have priority over light industry. The collectivisation drive has also been intensified, giving it some parallels with the Chinese 'Great Leap Forward'.

In Roumania, the economic position is similar to that of Bulgaria, although Roumania possesses important supplies of oil.

Albania, an inaccessible rural country with an area somewhat larger than Wales, has even less trade connections with countries outside the bloc. The reason for this is partly political, her Communist background being associated with Jugoslavia until the break in 1948. Since then, Albania's external relations have been bound yet closer to the bloc because of Jugoslav hostility. In these countries western foreign trade is a marginal residue of the economy.

7. Conclusion

The system of foreign trade is similar in all the European countries. It is modelled on the Soviet system. Orders have to be placed with the state import/export corporations, and they must be approved by the respective Ministry of Foreign Trade and come within the national economic plan. An exception to this rule is East Germany, which has not received diplomatic recognition from the western powers. By mutual consent, the practical arrangements are negotiated by the

East German Chamber of Trade, situated in East Berlin and acting on behalf of the East German Ministry of Foreign Trade.

To sum up, for purposes of western foreign trade, the east European countries vary in importance. In all of them, *Comecon* is playing an increasing part and its declared aim is to increase trade within the bloc rather than outside it. Nevertheless, opportunities for trade do exist, provided the markets are thoroughly studied and the products offered fit into the national plans.

Opportunities for contact are perhaps easier in Poland and Czechoslovakia than in the others. The great trade fairs, such as the one at Poznan—which began as exhibitions—are gradually taking on a trading rôle, and they pose a challenge to the initiative and diligence of the western business man.

K

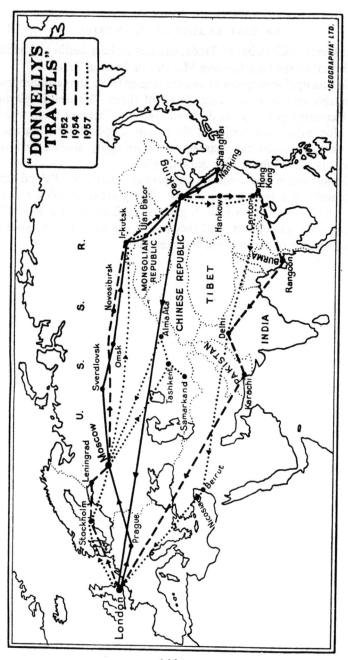

CHAPTER IV

China

1. *General*

The proclamation of the Chinese People's Republic on 1st October 1949 changed the government of nearly a quarter of mankind. Although it might never have happened without the Russian revolution, the Chinese revolution is of equal importance in the history of the world.

Thus, events in China have great implications for the west—economic as well as political. First, the transfer of political power to the Communists changed the whole pattern of trade in a market that, hitherto, had been very important to the United Kingdom. Very large British and foreign assets in China were taken over by the state, in stages. Then, the nature of the trade itself changed completely. Originally western countries had been conducting trade *in* China, from the revolution onwards it became trade *with* China.

Before turning to the practical details of the new pattern of trade, I must discuss briefly the background to the new Chinese political system and the points at which the conditions differ from those prevailing within the Soviet Union.

It has to be remembered that the Chinese Communist Party began in 1920 as an orthodox western Marxist-Leninist Party under Russian domination. Then, in 1927, there was a sudden change—imposed partly by events, partly by the physical problems of geography and lack of communications. Up to 1927, the Chinese Communists collaborated with Chiang Kai-shek. When Chiang felt strong enough, he took sudden steps to suppress them. Some of the Chinese Communist leaders were arrested and executed. Some fled

147

to Russia and yet others went underground. It was these latter who gathered round Mao Tse-tung and who led the long struggle for power which took them twenty-two years to win.

During the early period, following 1927, Mao's group was regarded with contempt in Moscow. Cut off from the outside world, Mao Tse-tung himself developed doctrines that were different from those supported by the Soviet Union. For a long period there was little association between the Communist parties of the two countries.

During World War II Stalin ignored the Chinese Communists and conducted all his dealings with Chiang Kai-shek. Even during the Chinese civil war which began in 1946 and ended in the Communist victory, paradoxically the Russian commitment on the Communist side was much less than the American support for Chiang Kai-shek.

It was only with the proclamation of the Communist government that the Soviet Union began to take the Chinese Communists seriously. And then, apart from the limited economic and political Sino-Soviet Treaty of 1950, it was still several years before there were signs of close collaboration. It really took the pressures of the total American embargo on all goods and technical facilities for China, following the outbreak of the Korean War, to give life to the Sino-Soviet alliance.

But still there was no association at top level. Mao Tse-tung made no move to visit Moscow whilst Stalin lived. It was five years before a top-ranking Soviet leader set foot in Peking. This was when Bulganin and Khrushchev led a delegation to China in September, 1954. From that visit onwards, economic co-operation became a reality.

There have also been overt signs again of political differences within the Sino-Soviet alliance, but these are outside the scope of this assessment, except in so far as they impinge upon trade.

The direct effect of American trade policy was to stimulate the Sino-Soviet alliance. Cut off from western technologies, Communist China had no alternative but to rely on the rest of the Soviet bloc. As a result, the country was visited continually by technicians from Russia, Czechoslovakia, East Germany and Poland. It is questionable whether China would have done otherwise in any event, but the fact remains that during the formative years of the Chinese revolution she was denied the opportunity to do anything else.

At this point it must be emphasised that, although China made use of Soviet bloc technicians, the formulation of economic policy remained firmly in Chinese hands. From this stemmed again the divergences of economic doctrine that have emerged from time to time, in particular the Great Leap Forward of 1958 and the drive for the Chinese Communes. Anxious to avoid the mistakes made by the Soviet Union in the 1920's and 1930's, China made her own mistakes.

The central problem of the Chinese economy remains her vast population growth. At present, the Chinese nation is growing at the rate of 12 to 15 millions every year. She already has a population of approximately 675 millions. By 1970 it may be 800 millions.

The economic problem thus posed for the Chinese Government is one of the greatest facing any government in recorded history. It is not merely a question of food supplies. *The real crux of the problem is the demand for capital formation at a sufficient speed to provide productive employment for upwards of twelve million people each year.*

At present and for some years to come, the only major source of new capital for China is agriculture. Her capacity to expedite her drive to industrialisation is dependent upon the ability of the Chinese peasant to pay for it. From year to year the economy is balanced on the outcome of the harvest. A bad harvest, as in 1956, causes severe stress within the economy. Two bad harvests in succession could cause crisis. The Chinese national economy remains extremely vulnerable not only to vicissitudes caused by the human factor but even to the vagaries of weather.

This weak internal economic position has enabled the Soviet Union to re-establish an economic and political leadership within the alliance. For instance, during the winter of 1958-9 the differences over the doctrine of the Communes and certain aspects of foreign policy were resolved by strong economic pressure upon China by Russia. Eventually China gave way on political and doctrinal issues, and in return the Soviet Union agreed to the new Sino-Soviet Economic Agreement of 1959 which involved a great increase in Russian economic assistance.

But the basic problems remain. In brief, it is a struggle between population and production. And for many years the outcome of the Chinese revolution will remain in doubt.

2. *The system*

The system for foreign trade with China is parallel to the system in other Communist countries. But there are certain differences.

First, the economy remains more centralised than in the Soviet Union. And until the economy becomes more highly developed, this greater centralisation will remain. There is a clear parallel for this in the history of the Soviet Union, in which the greater decentralisation only followed as the result of the increasing complexity of Soviet society.

Therefore, although the Ministry of Foreign Trade operates as in Russia, and all trade negotiations have to be conducted with the various state trade import/export corporations, the central Chinese Ministries have a more direct interest in industrial management than in Russia. To that extent, they play a part that in Russia is now devolved on to the *Sovnarkhozi* (see Book I, Part II, A). For this reason, a list of Chinese Ministries and other Government Departments interested in foreign trade is attached to the list of Chinese import/export corporations (see page 179).

All negotiations, as stated, have to be conducted with the import/export corporations. As with the Soviet Union, enquiries may begin with the Chinese representatives in London; but unlike the Soviet Union, China has no permanent trade delegation in Britain, although certain trade corporations claim to have officials attached to the office of the Chinese Commercial Counsellor. Sometimes, for negotiations of substance, it is necessary to negotiate with the Chinese mission at Berne, Switzerland. The reason for this is that the Chinese Legation at Berne is often used as a starting point for Chinese trade officials visiting western Europe. In all enquiries, however, the best starting point is at the office of the Chinese Commercial Counsellor in London, followed up by a letter direct to the appropriate import/export organisation in Peking.

Visits to Peking can be of great value and are appreciated by the Chinese authorities. However, individual firms should not undertake them without careful preparation and an assurance from the Chinese government that they are welcome. It must be emphasised that, if this is not done, the time and money expended may prove abortive.

Some firms employ agents already based in the Far East. Although the Chinese are no exception to the general rule of the Communist

bloc in their dislike of dealing with an agent, there are instances in
which such an arrangement has worked successfully, after the
Chinese authorities have been persuaded of its advantages and
relevance to the particular transaction or product.

All importation is the monopoly of the State Trading Corporations,
but these bodies have absorbed a number of the old Chinese merchant
importers, who (although now salaried employees of the Corporations
and wholly integrated with them) use their old names and notepaper
in their dealings with overseas suppliers.

Before early 1958, the usual form of payment used by the Chinese
authorities for their imports was an Irrevocable Letter of Credit
confirmed in London, with prompt payment on presentation of
documents. Then, from 1958 on, China began to ask for documentary
credits of 30 days. As time went on the period was extended, where
possible, to 60, 90 and in some cases 120 days.

Another change, from 1958 onwards, was the omission of the
Bank of China in London from the credit of confirmation. The effect
of this change was that in the event of non-payment, the exporter's
only redress was against the Bank of China in China.

There can be no clear generalisation about terms of payment. In
the last analysis, they are decided by negotiation and depend upon
the strength of the position of the seller.

3. *Travel arrangements*

Travel arrangements to Peking are relatively simple, but expensive.
A person from London can travel either via Moscow or Hong Kong.
A frequent jet service is in operation from Moscow to Peking and
the journey takes only a few hours. Bookings can be made through
any reputable travel agent. If travelling via Hong Kong, the visitor
has to break his air journey at Hong Kong and travel from the
Hong Kong border up to Canton by a slow train. From there, it is
possible to take the plane again to Peking.

Inside China, all arrangements have to be undertaken by Chinese
Intourist. The main hotels in cities such as Peking and Shanghai are
good. The prices, when compared with those in the Soviet Union,
are moderate. One important difference from the Russian practice
is that the services of an *Intourist* interpreter are not included in the
en pension Intourist charge. Instead, the interpreters are provided only

on request and are charged for separately. A word of caution regarding the cost of taxis in Peking is also necessary. Unlike other Chinese prices, taxi fares can be very expensive and the cost should be clearly ascertained before ordering. It is often much better to use a pedicab, which can be hired by the day for a small cost.

Travel facilities within the country are usually cleared only through the offices of the import or export corporation with whom the foreign business man is dealing. However, when such visits are advantageous to the Chinese authorities, arrangements can be made with great speed after periods of apparent inertia on their part.

4. *Chinese economic planning*

Following the revision of the targets or second Five Year Plan, which was drawn up in 1957, the Plan goes on and the Chinese authorities declare that it will be completed ahead of schedule.

Various sectors of the economy have had 'crash programmes' without any apparent regard to the overall balance of the economy. The result was the problems of transport and production that arose in 1959, in which there was grave dislocation. Many production targets were not fulfilled and had to be revised. But the authorities emphasise that the main Plan remains, and as stated it will in fact be completed ahead of schedule.

Under the Five Year Plan, the import priorities are broadly as follows:

1. Industrial materials, such as chemicals, finished steel, wool tops. Aids to increased agricultural production such as fertilisers and insecticides.
2. Specialised engineering products not made in China and not conveniently obtainable from the Soviet bloc.
3. Complete, or near complete, factories for products in which China's own development has so far been slow. Railway equipment, telecommunications equipment.
4. Light tractors and other agricultural equipment such as irrigation pumps.
5. Consumer goods; but here the opportunities are limited because of China's limited resources to pay.

CHAPTER V

Jugoslavia

The political background of Jugoslavia plays an important part in any understanding of her foreign trade position. First, unlike the other East European Communist countries, the Jugoslavian Communist Party led the fight for the liberation of the country in 1945 from German domination. Although there are differing opinions about the events that led up to the ending of the war in Jugoslavia, and of the respective values to the resistance movements of the Communist and the non-Communist forces, Marshal Tito emerged as the Jugoslav national leader in his own right. To that extent his government had a quite different internal status as compared with that of certain other East European governments.

When the break with the Soviet Union and the rest of the Communist bloc took place in 1948, it was Tito's own personal prestige which was largely responsible for enabling the Jugoslav Communist Government to survive; and it was the background of confidence, born out of the part that they themselves had played in the war against the Germans, that carried the Jugoslav Communist party through its ideological trauma.

During the seven years between 1948 and 1955, Jugoslavia remained a Communist country, with some ideological attitudes that became divergent from the main body of Marxist-Leninist doctrine. At that time, to be described as a 'Titoist' within the Communist bloc was sufficient to send a man to the gallows or to a firing squad—and many thousands perished in this way before Stalin's death. Furthermore, many more thousands were imprisoned for holding Titoist views or being suspected of holding them. I stress these points in

153

order to illustrate the gulf that grew up between Jugoslavia and the Communist bloc, and also to show the length to which Khrushchev went in his public apology to Tito at Belgrade airport in 1955.

As a result and for a short time, there was a rapprochement between Jugoslavia and the Communist bloc. But events in 1956, when 'Titoism' was overtly declared as the aim of many dissident Communists in Eastern Europe, re-opened old suspicions. The Jugoslav Communist party's refusal to accept policy as laid down in Moscow led to a renewal of the break. The hostility was not nearly so lethal on this occasion, however. Savage criticisms have been made from both sides, particularly by Chinese theoreticians who are on record as describing 'reformism' as the main enemy of Communist doctrine. But there the quarrel has ended—so far.

Jugoslavia remains a Communist country, outside the bloc, but not aligned with the western nations.

The consequence of these international and internal political vicissitudes is that Jugoslavia's foreign trade, within and without the Communist bloc, has fluctuated violently. Furthermore, in order to survive, the Tito Government has had to seek loans and assistance from western nations that would not have been permissible if Jugoslavia had remained an orthodox Communist country. The break with the bloc has also led to differences in internal Communist governmental theory and practice that express themselves clearly in Jugoslavian foreign trade.

1. The system

In consequence of the break with the Communist bloc the industrial and commercial organisation within Jugoslavia is more decentralised and liberal than in other Communist countries.

The system remains a planned economy, but central government planning is limited to broad annual plans and to decreeing laws to implement them. Financial control is exercised by the state banking organisation, consisting of the National Bank of Jugoslavia, the Investment Bank and the Jugoslav Bank for Foreign Trade (Jugobank). Although they are State-owned, all factories and other enterprises are independent of the Government in their day-to-day operations, provided they remain within the broad framework of the Central Plan. They have to act on their own initiative and to pay their way in competition with other publicly owned enterprises. The State encourages this kind of enterprise by allowing each firm to retain a proportion of its profits, partly for re-investment and partly for distribution amongst the employees.

Unlike other Communist countries, the Jugoslav Government permits certain state concerns to undertake import and export business on their own, provided they can satisfy the central authority that they are competent to do so. On this basis some of the larger factories import their requirements, although their permits are usually limited to products of which they are in regular need. For non-recurring imports the normal procedure is to channel the trade through one of the recognised import trading organisations.

The larger import organisations cover the whole country. The smaller ones are usually restricted to the districts in which they are situated. This method is clearly another substantial departure from the practice of the other Communist countries.

The import trading organisations however follow the general Communist pattern of not being, themselves, responsible for stimulating the demands of their consumers. Whilst they state that they welcome enquiries from foreign firms, at the same time they have no power to place business unless they have received an order from one of their 'clients'. Their responsibility is to sign contracts on behalf of their 'client' with the foreign firms offering the best terms as to price, quality and delivery date.

Exporting enterprises operate in a similar manner and their allocation of functions is also the same in relation to their size and the district in which they are situated.

A directory with the names and addresses of all export/import organisations classified, both alphabetically and under subject headings is published by:

The Federal Chamber of Foreign Trade,
12 Mosa Pijade,
Belgrade.

Jugoslavia's main imports consist of raw materials and complex kinds of capital equipment; but since 1956 there has been an annual allocation of foreign exchange for the import of consumer goods.

At this point there is another break with orthodox Communist practice. The original system of issuing import and export licences which followed decentralisation has been abolished and replaced by a system of 'co-efficients' (in effect, import taxes and export subsidies) designed (1) to conceal the difference between Jugoslav domestic prices and world prices, (2) to impose a desired pattern on overseas trade by discouraging the import of inessentials and (3) to protect certain home industries. These co-efficients, sometimes referred to as 'factors', replace ordinary customs duties.

Import licences as such have been abolished, but the state import organisations have to obtain special permits from the appropriate Government Department for the import of the following categories of goods:

(a) all finished machinery and equipment, parts and spare parts of equipment, machines, apparatus and vehicles purchased by the metal processing, electrical and ship-building industries for incorporation into finished products.

(b) all manufactured consumer goods.

(c) all motor vehicles, with the exception of passenger cars and motor cycles obtained by individuals as gifts or purchased from earnings abroad.

In deciding whether to grant applications for these permits, the authorities take into consideration whether the goods in question are already made in the country in sufficient quantities or in the required quality, and whether they still could be made internally under manufacturing agreements with foreign firms. This means that the market for most goods already produced in Jugoslavia is either closed or limited, and foreign manufacturers who conclude local licensing agreements have certain advantages. For example, the assembly plant established in Jugoslavia by Massey-Ferguson has given this firm an important position in the tractor market.

A number of foreign firms use Jugoslav state-owned enterprises as their agents. This is the corollary to greater autonomy of all industrial organisations and the need to influence their choice of products by personal contact and sales promotion. Such agencies do not import on their own account; their main function is to bring foreign firms into contact with consumers. They can undertake to effect sales on behalf of foreign firms and to perform after-sales technical services. They can also hold consignment stocks on behalf of foreign firms.

Foreign firms cannot employ private individuals, either foreign or Jugoslav, as resident agents, but they can, of course, seek to promote sales by visits to the country.

Details of the authorised agency enterprises are obtainable from the Federal Chamber of Trade (see page 155).

2. *General*

Since Jugoslavia has suffered from a chronic shortage of foreign exchange, much of her foreign trade has been financed by means of Government-to-Government credits or loans. For example, in 1959, the United Kingdom Government granted Jugoslavia a loan of £3 millions. In return the Jugoslav Government furnished the Board of Trade with a list of prospective purchases.*

The Export Credit Guarantees Department also is prepared to grant cover on certain sales to Jugoslavia. UK exporters who consider granting credit should examine the possibility of having it guaranteed by the National Bank of Jugoslavia.

* These are not reproduced here because of the time factor involved and the difficulty of checking the accuracy of all transactions that have taken place since, but the Export Services Branch of the Board of Trade will be ready to answer enquiries.

The Prospects for East-West Trade

East-West trade has developed steadily, if slowly, since the 1952 Moscow Economic Conference. The easement in foreign travel that followed Stalin's death has helped. With the exception of journeys to China, it has become much easier for western business men to travel to Communist countries. For their part, more and more citizens of the Communist bloc have come west. They have seen for themselves how westerners live and been able to measure western technological progress.   Another and even more important factor in stimulating East-West trade has been the great drive for industrial expansion in most countries of the Communist bloc and their resulting demand for western capital goods.

The pattern of these changes has been outlined broadly in these pages. But what of the future?

The world is moving into an era of new relationships with the powers of the Communist bloc. This is the direct result of the military stalemate that developed in the late 1950's; and the growing acceptance—by both sides—of the consequences of nuclear war. It is also due, in part, to the enormous strides made by Soviet industry and technology, which is changing the balance of economic power in the world at an astonishing rate.

The realisation by the Soviet leaders of the futility of attempting world conquest for Communism by military force has been hailed as an event of profound importance. This is true. But it is quite wrong to go on from there to assume that the basic aims of Communism are changing. Naturally it can be argued that the fires of the revolution are burning lower as Russian Communists of third generation grow up to accept positions of responsibility—for them, there is a change. But for Khrushchev and his immediate circle the basic aims have not changed. They still believe that one day the whole world will be Communist. They still consider that it is their mission in life to further this end, to the best of their ability and to the limit of their strength.

The real change of the 1960's for the Communist leadership is the shift in emphasis from military pressures on the boundaries of the Communist world to political and economic competition in selected areas—'Competitive Co-existence', as Mr Khrushchev himself calls it.

What is the implication of the new era for the peoples who dwell in the West and who do not accept the Communist way of life? First, we must understand that Khrushchev is really stating that there is to be a reversal of the saying 'trade follows the flag'. In Khrushchev's view, ideas and political influence will now follow in the wake of trade—on his terms. Hence the vital importance of East-West trade in the next ten years.

The Communist concept of foreign trade is different from our own —as I have already made clear. For them, the priorities are different. Fundamentally their's is an over-riding political aim, and so it will remain until the dynamic of the revolution expends itself with the passage of time—or until the Communist victory envisaged by Khrushchev is achieved.

Within this framework of thinking, the Communists' first aim is to strengthen the bloc, either by adding to its industrial strength or by binding closer the economic ties. Their second aim is to expand their economic influence outside the bloc. Thereby they hope to bring more countries under Communist influence, and eventually under Communist control.

The Communist leadership has had to accept a major calculated risk before it could embark upon this policy. This risk is the likely effect on the minds of the Communist peoples themselves of greater contact with peoples outside—the corollary of increased contacts by trade.

The result is a new challenge to western civilisation. Which is the better economic system? Which makes for the better life and for quicker rises in living standards?

We have to recognise that the Communist bloc possesses certain advantages. First, its centralised control and political autocracy enables the leadership to concentrate capital investment more easily at the strategic points of the economy. This has led to spectacular progress, as has been shown by Soviet achievements in space research. Equally it has developed the formidable Russian machine-tool industry, which now threatens the western position in the markets of the world.

Secondly, the rigid political control that exists over the bloc's economy also means that, for a time, export prices and terms of trade can be used to serve political ends. This is an adaptation of the foreign trade policy deployed by Hitler in the 1930's. The specific danger here is that the resources of the bloc are always sufficient to place any individual western industrialist at a hopeless disadvantage and the West must find a way of countering.

Thirdly, the Communist countries have always shown that they are prepared to use the offer of large contracts to stimulate pressures within western countries—for Communist ends. Sometimes these contracts never materialise. They are used merely to whet appetites in one country after another.

These factors add up to a formidable political and economic problem that is now posed to the West. On the other hand, the West also has its advantages. The Achilles heel of the Communist bloc is the spirit of their own peoples. There are very few Communists within the East European countries. A notable feature of the years 1945-1960 has been the failure of the Communist education system to change this situation. In the Soviet Union itself, there are parallel failures. For instance, it is the new generation of students who are questioning the fundamentals of Communist dogma and demanding greater freedoms of speech. Khrushchev himself realises this only too clearly. For this specific reason he has led the movement for controlled liberalisation within the bloc; but the question that only history can answer is whether such liberalisation, once started, can be controlled.

Only in China is the political pattern still so rigid that it is almost impossible to evoke an answering response. There are reasons of race and history for this difference in the Far East; in particular, it is that China is still in her Stalinist phase of the revolution. The barriers that surrounded the Russia of the 1930s now stand around

L

China in the early 1960s. Added to this are the population pressures I have outlined earlier, and the dangers that are implicit in them.

The task of western countries is therefore clear. It is to use the instrument of trade not only to meet the Communist challenge on neutral territories in Africa and Asia but also to take their own economic challenge into the most remote cities of the Soviet Union itself.

We are only at the beginning of the possibilities for ingenuity and resource that can help to establish contact with the peoples who dwell east of the River Elbe. If we develop our East-West trade, it will have a profound effect on the course of political history. If we stand negative and passive, we shall court disaster. The choice is largely our own, not only for governments but right down to the level of the individual business man: from now on he is in the front line of the ideological and political struggle for the world.

Part II

Trading Corporations
and the commodities they handle

A. SOVIET UNION

Notes: 1. Unless otherwise stated, the address is: 32/34, Smolenskaya-Sennaya, Moscow G-200.

2. Except where otherwise designated, the corporations import and export, even though the name suggests only one or the other.

MACHINOEXPORT (export only)
Power, electro-technical, mining, transportation and material handling, chemical, food and light (e.g. textile) industrial equipment.

AVTOEXPORT (export only)
Automobiles, tractors, agricultural machinery, gauges and measuring equipment.

TECKHNOPROMIMPORT (import only)
Equipment for the chemical, building, timber, paper, food, light rubber and printing industries; automobiles, tractors, agriculture machinery; telegraph, telephone and radio equipment; gauges and measuring equipment and laboratory equipment.

STANKOIMPORT
Machine tools, forging and stamping machines, instruments, ball-bearings, measuring machines, hard alloys, abrasives, cinema equipment, optical apparatus.

SUDOIMPORT
Ships, ship repairs and refitting.

PROMSYRIEMIMPORT
Rolling mill products, railway equipment, ferro-alloys, special steels, pipes.

RAZNOIMPORT
Non-ferrous metals, rubber, rubber goods.

EXPORTLES   6, *ul, Kuibysheva, Moscow-Centre.*
Timber of all kinds, pulp and paper, etc.

SOYUZPROMEXPORT
Products of the mining and fuel industries, fertilisers.

SOYUZXHIMEXPORT
Chemical and medicinal products.

SOYUZNEFTEXPORT
Oil and oil products.

SOYUZPUSHNINA   37, *Donskaya, Moscow V-49.*
Raw furs, semis and manufactures, bristles, horsehair, carpets.

EXPORTKHLEB
Grain, pulses, oilseeds, oilcake, bran, seeds.

EXPORTLEN
Raw cotton, wool, flax, fibres, cloth, etc.

PRODINTORG
Foodstuffs (other than those listed under Exportkhleb), live animals.

RAZNOEXPORT 5, *Kalyayevskaya, Moscow K-6.*
Tobacco and manufactures, raw animal products, leather goods, building materials, etc.

TSENTROSOYUZ (Consumer co-operatives) *Bolshoi Cherkasskii pereulok*, 15/17 *Moscow.*
Wide range of commodities, principally foodstuffs and consumers' goods. (Generally undertakes only small-scale bilaterally-balanced deals.)

MEZHDUNARODNAYA KNIGA
Books, periodicals, music, reproductions, stamps, musical equipment, paintings.

SOVEXPORTFILM   7, *Maly Gnezdnikovsky, Moscow K-104.*
Cinema films.

VOSTOKINTORG   37, *Donskaya, Moscow, V-49.*
Various commodities in trade with Mongolia, the Sinkiang area of China, Afghanistan and Iran.

MACHINOIMPORT
(import only) Power, electro-technical, oil, mining, transport and materials, moving equipment.
(export and import) Railway rolling stock.

SOVFRAKHT   4, *Pr. Vladimirova, Moscow K-12.*
Chartering of ships, forwarding, transport of goods, transit.

AFTOVNESHTRANS
Road and river transportation of goods between USSR and China, Mongolia, Afghanistan and Iran.

VNESHTORGIZDAT *Oruzheinyi Pereulok 25a, Moscow D-47.*
Publication of books, periodicals and advertising matter on foreign trade.

INTOURIST   1, *ul. Gorky, Moscow K-9.*
Tourism (of foreigners in the USSR and of Soviet citizens abroad).

TEKHNOEXPORT			Delivery of complete factor-
TEKHNOPROMEXPORT	Export		ies, technical aid, research and
TYAZHPROMEXPORT	only		quantity surveying work
PROMMASHEXPORT			abroad.

Source: P. A. Chervyakov: *Organizatsia i Tekhnika Vneshnei Torgovli SSSR.* (Moscow, 1958), p.41.

(*Note:* The precise designations and coverage are liable to amendment from time to time.)

B. POLAND

ANIMEX. *Warszawa, Pulawska 14.*
Exports and imports livestock, animal products, fish and fish products

ARS POLONA. *Warszawa, Krakowskie, Przedmescie 7.*
Exports and imports periodicals, books, music, postage stamps for collectors, works of art.

BALTONA. *Gdynia, Pulaskiego 6.*
Ship chandlers.

CEKOP. *Warszawa, Mokotowska, 49.*
Exports plant equipment and complete factory installations.

C. HARTWIG LTD. *Warszawa, Przemyslowa 26.*
International forwarding agents.

CENTRALA MORSKA. *Warszawa, Mokotowska, 49.*
Imports and exports merchant ships and fishing gear, shipyard and ship's equipment.

CENTROZAP. *Katowice, Plebiscytowa, 36.*
Imports and exports capital plant and equipment for the mining, iron and steel industries, foundry and rolling mill equipment, cranes and conveyors, rails, pipes, steel sheets, zinc and rolled zinc products.

CETEBE. *Lodz, Narutowicza, 13.*
Exports and imports textiles and clothing.

CIECH, *Warszawa, Jasna 12.*
Exports and imports chemicals and products of the chemical industry.

COOPEXIM. *Spoldzielcze Przedsiebiorstwo Handlu Zagranicznego, Warszawa, Zurawia, 4.*
Imports raw materials and machinery required by Polish Co-operatives. Exports the products of consumers', artisans', handicraft workers' and invalids' co-operatives.

DAL. *Warszawa, Frascati 2.*
Barter and re-export transactions.

168   TRADE WITH COMMUNIST COUNTRIES

ELEKTRIM. *Warszawa, Czackiego* 15/17.
Imports and exports power plant, electrical machinery and equipment;
radio and telecommunication equipment, electrical measuring instruments, electrical accessories and cables.

FABEX. *Warszawa, Krucza* 18/20.
Exports concrete making plant.

PAGED. *Warszawa, Pl. Trzech Krzyzy* 18.
Exports and imports timber, sawn timber and products of the woodworking industry, paper, stationery and office appliances.

HORTEX. *Warszawa, Warecka* 11a.
Exports fresh and canned fruit and vegetables, honey and early potatoes.

FILMOW. *Warszawa, Marszalkowska* 56.
Imports, exports, and hires, films.

IMPEXMETAL. *Warszawa, Wilcza* 50/52.
Imports and exports non-ferrous metals, alloys and rolling bearings.

METAL EXPORT. *Warszawa, Mokotowska,* 49.
Exports machine tools, woodworking machinery; sugar work's plant;
plant for the textile and paper industry; contractors' plant. Exports
and imports rolling stock and cast-iron and steel products.

MINEX. *Warszawa, Krakowskie Przedmiexcie* 79.
Exports and imports glass, chinaware, ceramics, building and insulation
materials, cement and minerals.

MOTOIMPORT. *Warszawa, Przemyzlowa,* 26.
Imports and exports motor vehicles, agricultural machinery and
implements.

PETROLIMPEX. *Warszawa, Jasna,* 12.
Exports and imports petroleum and allied products.

P.Z.U. *Warszawa, Traugutta,* 5.
Conducts all classes of insurance, including marine.

POLCARGO. *Gdynia, Pulaskiego,* 6.
Cargo measurement, weight, quantity and quality checks.

POLCOOP. *Warszawa, Kopernika* 30.
Office of the Central Agricultural Union of the Peasants' Self-Help
Co-operative. Exports agricultural products; imports agricultural
machinery and products.

POLFRACHT. *Gdynia, P.O.B.* 206.
Shipbrokers, chartering agents, freight contractors, managers of
t/c tonnage.

POLIMEX. *Warszawa, Czackiego* 7/9/11.
Imports machine tools, plant and equipment for plastic machining.
stone and ore crushers, pumps, compressors, plant and equipment
for the chemical, foods, woodworking, building and other industries,

PRODIMEX. *Warszawa, Miodowa*, 14.
Imports materials and fittings for handicrafts on behalf of small manufacturing co-operatives, e.g. suitcase locks, fittings and handles, etc.

ROLIMPEX. *Warszawa, Zurawia* 32/34.
Export and import of cereals, industrial plants, sugar and seeds.

SKORIMPEX. *Lodz, 22 Lipca No.* 74.
Import and export of hides and skins, furs, as well as leather and rubber goods.

SPOLEM. *Warszawa, Grazyny* 13.
Office of the Union of Consumers Co-operatives. Imports groceries and spices; exports and barters food products.

TEXTILIMPORT. *Lodz, 22 Lipca* 8.
Exports and imports textile raw materials of vegetable, animal and synthetic origin.

UNIVERSAL. *Warszawa, ul. Wspolna* 3/5 *or ul. Hoza* 20.
Exports durable consumer goods, such as radio and television sets, metal kitchenware, household appliances, musical instruments, watches and sports goods.

WEGLOKOKS. *Katowice-Welnowiec, Armii Czerwonej* 119.
Exports coal and coke.

VARIMEX. *Warszawa, Wilcza* 50/52.
Imports, exports scientific and laboratory apparatus, measuring instruments, plant and equipment for the textile, printing, and leather industries, and sports equipment.

C. CZECHOSLOVAKIA

STATE TRADING ORGANISATIONS

FERROMET: 27, *Opletalova, Praha,* 11, *P.O. B.*799. *Czechoslovakia.*
Tel. 2363-07, 2331-50, 2208-41.
Export and import of metallurgical products.

STROJEXPORT: 56 *Vaclavsko nam., Praha-Czechoslovakia.*
Tel. 246850, 248850.
Export of machines and machinery equipment.

STROJIMPORT: *Prague II, Vaclavske, nam.* 56. *Tel.* 240850, 245041-9.
Import of machinery and industrial equipment.

MOTOKOV: 47, *Tr. Dukelskych Hrdinu, Praha VII, Czechoslovakia.*
Tel. 0000, 786-40/9, 732-40/9.
Import and export of vehicles and light engineering products and aeroplanes.

OMNIPOL, LTD.: *Washingtonova* 11, *Praha* 3.
Export of aeroplanes and sports equipment.

M

KOVO: 47 *Tr. Dukelskych Hrdinu, Praha VII, Czechoslovakia. Tel.* 0000, 741-41/45.
Import and export of precision engineering products.

CHEMAPOL: 9 *Panska, Praha* 11, *Czechoslovakia. Tel.* 2279-44/7, 2217-50, 2245-93.
Import and export of chemical products and raw materials.

CZECHOSLOVAK CERAMICS: 1 *V Jame, Praha* 11, *Czechoslovakia. Tel.* 2477-40-49.
Export and import of Ceramic ware.

GLASSEXPORT: 1 *Vaclavskenam., P.O.B.* 795, *Praha* 11, *Czechoslovakia. Tel.* 2432-51.
Export of glass.

JABLONEX: 12, *Gottwaldova, Jablonec Nad Nisou, Czechoslovakia. Tel.* 2851-4.
Export of Jablonec articles.

LIGNA: 41, *Vodickova, Praha* 11, *Czechoslovakia.*
Export and import of timber and products of the woodworking and paper industries.

PRAGO-EXPORT: 34, *Jungmannova, Praha* 11, *Czechoslovakia.*
Export and import of smallware and outfitting articles.

CENTROTEX: 47, *Trida Dukelskych Hrdinu, Praha VII, P.O. B.*7970, *Czechoslovakia.*
Import and export of textiles and leather goods.

KOOSPOL: 47, *Trida Dukelskych Hrdinu, Praha VII, Czechoslovakia.*
Import and export of agricultural products and implements.

CENTROKOMISE: 5, *Konviktska, Praha I, Czechoslovakia.*
Import and export of foodstuffs.

ARTIA: 30, *Smecky, Praha II, Czechoslovakia.*
Exporters—importers of cultural commodities.

METALIMEX: *Prague II, Stepanska* 34. *Tel.* 2235-51/5, 2268-53.
Import and export of ores, metals, and solid fuels.

TECHNOEXPORT: *Prague II, Vaclavske nam.* 56. *Tel.* 244850, 245041-9
Export of complete industrial plant.

CECHOFRACHT: *Prague* 1, *Prikopy* 1. *Tel..* 2272-45.
Corporation for shipping.

METRANS: *Prague I, Prikopy* 8. *Tel.* 2403-41, 2216-41, 2267-55.
Corporation for international forwarding.

INVESTA LIMITED: *Prague II, Vaclavske nam.* 56, (*P.O.B.* 662), (*Head Office*) *Tel.* 2448-51, 2468-51, 2488-51.
Heavy engineering products, import and export company.

D. ROUMANIA

AGROEXPORT: *Bucharest, Str. Doamnei No. 12, POB.* 141. *Tel.* 16.10.81.
Exports grain, general agricultural products, tobacco, cigarettes, medicinal herbs. Imports all kinds of seeds for growing and industrialization purposes.

CARTIMEX: *Bucharest, Str. A. Briand Nr.* 14-18, *P.O.B.* 134-135. *Tel.* 15.96.49.
Exports and imports newspapers, periodicals and books.

CHIMIMPORT: *Bucharest, Str. Doamnei No.* 12, *P.O.B.* 525. *Tel.* 16.06.36
Exports and imports chemicals.

DIFILM: *Bucharest, Str. Julius Fucic Nr.* 25. *Tel.* 11.13.08.
Exports and imports films.

EXPORTLEMN: *Bucharest, Piata Rosetti Nr.* 4, *P.O.B.* 802. *Tel.* 16.29.63
Exports and imports wood products, newsprint and furniture.

INDUSTRIALEXPORT: *Bucharest, Str. Gabriel Peri Nr.* 2. *P.O.B.* 101. *Trunk calls* 116.
Exports and imports engineering products including machine tools and electrical appliances.

MASINIMPORT: *Bucharest, Str. Mihail Eminescu No.* 10. *P.O.B.* 3008. *Tel.* 12.54.25.
Exports rolling stock, steam, diesel and electric locomotives, passenger cars, freight trucks, tank-cars, motor-coaches. River- and sea-going vessels up to 4,000 tons. Complete electric power plants. Imports machines and equipment for metallurgy of iron, building material and wood industries, cellulose and paper industry, foodstuff industry, refrigerating and freezing plants, leather and footwear industries, chemical and pharmaceutical industries, rubber, plastics and allied industries, textile industry, ships, nautical engines and outfits, rolling stock and railway accessories, electric power plants.

METALIMPORT: *Bucharest, Bd. 6 Martie Nr.* 42. *Tel.* 14.88.91.
Exports non-ferrous metals. Imports pig-iron, ferro-alloys, scrap iron, rolled and drawn ordinary and alloyed steel, non-ferrous metals in blocks or rolled, electric coil wire.

PETROLEXPORT: *Bucharest, Bd. 6 Martie Nr.* 42. *Tel.* 15.70.17.
Exports and imports oils and related products.

PRODEXPORT: *Bucharest, Str. Gabriel Peri Nr.* 5-7. *P.O.B.* 122. *Tel.* 15.97.30.
Exports live animals for slaughter and breeding, sturgeon fish preserves, caviar, cheeses and preserves, wines and spirits. Imports colonial products and spices, animals for breeding, products and by-products for alimentary use.

PUBLICOM: *Bucharest, Bul. N. Balcescu No. 22; Tel. 15.24.29.*
Roumanian Publicity Agency.

ROMANOEXPORT: *Bucharest, Piata Rosetti Nr. 4. Tel. 14.35.96.*
Exports furs, leather goods, building and furniture materials. Imports
all kinds of animal, vegetable and synthetic textiles, hides, skins and
leather goods and tanning materials.

ROMTRANS: *Bucharest, calea Rahovei Nr. 196; Oficiul Lenin P.O.B.*
6022. *Tel. 6.21.10.*
This is the State company for international transport and forwarding;
it carries out all operations in connection with the international forwarding of import, export and transit goods (chartering and agency services
for Roumanian or foreign ships).

TECHNOIMPORT: *Bucharest, Str. Doamnei Nr. 5. P.O.B.* 110.
Tel. 16.45.70.
Imports engineering products such as aircraft, motor vehicles, motor
cycles, bicycles, printing machinery and equipment, industrial control
and measuring apparatus, office machines, electric meters and laboratory
apparatus.

E. BULGARIA

BULGARPLODEXPORT: 1, *Ivan Vazov St., Sofia. Tel. 7-51-51.*
Exports fresh, dried and frozen fruits and vegetables, jams, wines,
liqueurs, brandies, and molasses. Imports fresh and dried fruits.

BULGARTABAK: 1, *Dobrudja St., Sofia. Tel. 8-49-34.*
Exports tobacco and cigarettes.

CHIMINMPORT: 2, *Stefan Kavadja St., Sofia. Tel. 8-38-11, 12, 13, 14.*
Exports chemicals, fertilizers, pharmaceutical products. Imports
chemicals, fertilizers, insecticides, raw rubber and rubber articles,
dyes, lacquer and pigments, photographic films and papers, essential
oils, shellac, medical and dental instruments and articles.

HRANEXPORT: 2, *A. Kunchev St., Sofia. Tel. 8-22-51.*
Exports grain, sugar, bristles, animal food products, live animals.
Imports colonial goods, spices, wax, live animals, fish.

INDUSTRIALIMPORT: 3, *Pozitano St., Sofia. Tel. 7-30-21.*
Exports textile goods. Imports textile raw materials, tyres, cotton
and woollen piece goods and piece goods of man-made fibres.

METALIMPORT: 2, *Slavianska St., Sofia. Tel. 7-43-21.*
Exports and imports electrical and non-electrical machinery and
precision instruments.

PETROL: 11*th August St., Sofia,* 6. *Tel. 8-09-21.*
Exports crude oil. Imports various petroleum products.

RAZNOIZNOS: 1, *Tsar Assen* 1 *St., Sofia. Tel.* 8-02-11.
Exports industrial semi-manufactures other than metals.   Imports durable consumer goods and printed matter.

RUDMETAL: 1, *Dobfudja St., Sofia. Tel.* 8-12-71.
Exports ores, concentrates, metals (in ingot and sheet form), minerals, construction materials and coal. Imports ferrous and non-ferrous metals and products, cables and minerals.

TECHNOIMPEX: 2, *Slavianska St., Sofia. Tel.* 7-43-21 or 8-49-91.
Imports complete factories, installations or plant for various industries including mining, building and construction, chemical, food, power and electrical engineering industries.

F. CHINA

China National Sundries Export Corporation

Principal Exports and Imports: Raw cotton, cotton piece-goods and cotton yarn, cotton knitwear and manufactured goods, ramie and woollen goods (gunny bags excepted), glass and glassware, sundry goods for daily use, paper, stationery and educational supplies, musical instruments, toys, sports goods, glazed wall tiles, plywood, asphalt roofing felt, asbestos products, household electrical supplies and sanitary wares, etc.

	Address	*Cable Address*
Head Office:	*Tung An Men Street, Peking*	SUNDRY PEKING
Shanghai Branch:	128, *Hu Chiu Road, Shanghai*	SUNDRY SHANGHAI
Tientsin Branch:	114, *Ta Ku Road, Tientsin*	SUNDRY TIENTSIN
Canton Branch:	2, *Chiaw Kwang Road, Canton*	SUNDRY CANTON
Tsingtao Branch:	10, *Tientsin Road, Tsingtao*	SUNDRY TSINGTAO
Shanghai Stationery and Educational Supplies Import and Export Corporation	128, *Hu Chiu Road, Shanghai*	STATIONERY SHANGHAI
Shanghai Toys Import & Export Corporation	128, *Hu Chiu Road, Shanghai*	CHINATOYS SHANGHAI
Shanghai Textile Export Corporation	27, *Chung Shan Road, E.*1. *Shanghai.*	TEXTILE SHANGHAI

China National Native Produce Export Corporation

Principal Exports and Imports: Bast fibre and its manufactures, tobacco and its manufactures, various kinds of native products, wood and timber, nuts, dried vegetables and subsidiary foodstuffs, arts and crafts, porcelains and pottery, medicines and patent medicines, spices, essential oils, etc.

	Address	Cable Address
Head Office:	Tung An Men Street, Peking	PROCHINA PEKING
Peking Branch:	1, Hsi Chiao Min Hsiang, Peking	PEKARTCO PEKING
Peking Arts and Crafts Co.	1 Hsi Chiao Min Hsiang, Peking	PEKARTCO PEKING
Tientsin Branch:	33, Harbin Road, Tientsin	NCNPC TIENTSIN
Tientsin Arts and Crafts Export Corporation	33 Harbin Road, Tientsin	ARTS TIENTSIN
Tsingtao Branch:	14, Paoting Road, Tsingtao	CNPCO TSINGTAO
Shanghai Branch:	16, Chung Shan Road, E.1. Shanghai	CHINAPROCO SHANGHAI
Shanghai Arts and Crafts Export Corporation:	29 Chung Shan Road, E.1. Shanghai	ARTSCRAFT SHANGHAI
Fukien Branch:	Foreign Trade Building, East Street, Foochow	PROFUKIEN FOOCHOW
Canton Branch:	282, Dah Teh Road, Canton	PROCANTON CANTON
Canton Arts and Crafts Export Corporation:	125, Tai Ping Road, Canton	ARTCANTON CANTON
Canton Ceramics Export Company:	109, Tien Cheng Road, Canton	CERAMICO CANTON
Canton Native Medicines Export Corporation:	502, Yih Teh Road, Canton	CNMEC CANTON
Kwangsi Branch:	11, Tsinan Road, Nanning	PRONANNING NANNING
Hongkong Agency Teck Soon Hong Ltd.:	37-39 Connaught Road, West, Hongkong	STILLON HONGKONG

China National Animal By-products Export Corporation

Principal Exports and Imports: Bristles, horsetails, fur, fur plates, skins, hides, feathers, casings, wool, cashmere, hairs, carpets, brushes, leather and leather products, fur products, wooltops, living animals, etc.

	Address	Cable Address
Head Office:	Tung An Men Street, Peking	BYPRODUCTS PEKING
Shanghai Branch:	23, Chung Shan Road, E.1. Shanghai	BYPRODUCTS SHANGHAI
Tientsin Branch:	66, Yen Tai Street, Tientsin	BYPRODUCTS TIENTSIN
Canton Branch:	486, Liu Erh San Road, Canton	BYPRODUCTS CANTON
Tsingtao Branch:	24, Hupeh Road, Tsingtao	BYPRODUCTS TSINGTAO

China National Foodstuffs Export Corporation

Principal Exports and Imports: Live stock and poultry, frozen meat and meat products, frozen poultry, frozen game, frozen edible animal by-products, aquatic and marine products, eggs and egg products, canned goods of fish, meat, poultry, fruits and vegetables, fresh fruits and vegetables, beer, liquors and wines, aerated water, fruit juice and jams, preserved or dried fruits, confections, biscuits, sugar, etc.

	Address	*Cable Address*
Head Office:	*Tung An Men Street, Peking*	FOODSTUFFS PEKING
Shanghai Branch:	26, *Chung Shan Road, E.1.*	
	Shanghai	CHINAFOOCO SHANGHAI
Tientsin Branch:	134, *Chih Feng Road, Hoping Chu,*	
	Tientsin	FOODSTUFFS TIENTSIN
Tsingtao Branch:	18 *Chung Shan Road, Tsingtao*	FOODSTUFFS TSINGTAO
Canton Branch:	137, *Taiping Road, Canton*	FOODCO CANTON
Fukien Branch:	94, *Tung Chieh Road, Foochow*	5028 FOOCHOW
Kwangsi Branch:	11, *Tsinan Road, Nanning*	1795 NANNING
Hupeh Provincial Branch:	87, *The Bund, Hankow*	FOODSTUFFS HANKOW
Hunan Provincial Import & Export Corporation:	2, *Wu-l East Road, Changsha*	5752 CHANGSHA
Hongkong Agency NG Fung Hong:	*Bank of China Buildings,*	
	Hongkong	NGFUNG, HONGKONG

China National Cereals, Oils and Fats Exports Corporation

Principal Exports and Imports: Cereals (rice, wheat, horse beans, broad beans, pulses, etc.), Oil seeds (soya beans, groundnut kernels, sesameseed, linseed, rapeseed, copra, etc.), Oils (wood oil, groundnut oil, cottonseed oil, tea oil, cocoanut oil, etc.), salt, etc.

	Address	*Cable Address*
Head Office:	*Tung An Men Street, Peking*	NATIONOIL PEKING
Shanghai Branch:	*Bank of China Building,*	
	Shanghai	CHINAFAT SHANGHAI
Tientsin Branch	80, *Chu Fu Road, Tientsin*	NOIL TIENTSIN
Canton Branch:	1, *Yung Han Road North,*	CNCOFC CANTON
	Canton	
Tsingtao Branch:	29, *Wu Sung Road, Tsingtao.*	NACEROIL TSINGTAO

China National Tea Export Corporation

Exports and Imports: Black tea, green tea, oolong tea, white tea, scented tea, compressed tea, coffee, cocoa.

	Address	*Cable Address*
Head Office:	*Tung An Men Street, Peking*	NATIONTEA PEKING
Shanghai Branch:	74, *Tien Chih Road, Shanghai*	NATIONTEA SHANGHAI

Kwangtun
  Branch: 486, *Liu Erh San Road, Canton*   NATIONTEA CANTON
Fukien Branch: *Foreign Trade Building,*   NATIONTEA FOOCHOW
                       East Street, Foochow
Amoy Office: *Foreign Trade Building,*   NATIONTEA AMOY
                       Hai Hou Road, Amoy
Swatow Office: 88, *Sheng Ping Road, Swatow*   NATIONTEA SWATOW

China National Minerals Corporation

Principal Exports and Imports: Coal, cement, pig iron, pyrolusite, pyrolusite in powder, tin, antimony regulus, antimony white, magnesite, dolomite in powder, fluorspar, bauxite, clay, talc, talc powder, graphite, Barite, alum, gypsum, china clay, feldspar, calcite, diatomaceous earth, bentonite, realgar, orpiment, arsenic oxide, limestone, vermiculite, mineral colours, ballstone, quartz, chrome ore, mica, etc.

	Address	*Cable Address*
Head Office:	3, *Pao Chan Sze Street, Peking*	CHIMINCORP PEKING
Tientsin Branch:	2, *Jung Te Li, Hopei South Road, Tientsin*	CNMCTBO TIENTSIN
Tsingtao Branch:	9, *Tang Yi Road, Tsingtao*	CNMC TSINGTAO
Shanghai Branch:	16, *Chung Shan Road, E.1. Shanghai*	MINERALS SHANGHAI
Kwangtun Branch:	56, *West Bund, Canton*	CHIMINCORP CANTON
Kwangsi Branch:	11, *Tsinan Road, Nanning, Kwangsi*	CNMCKB NANNING
Fukien Branch:	*Foreign Trade Building, East Street, Foochow*	MINERALS FOOCHOW

China National Silk Corporation

Principal Exports and Imports: Raw silk steam filature, douppion silk, tussah silk, spun silk yarn and silk tops, silk waste and tussah silk waste, pure and mixed silk piece-goods, tussah silk pongees, fuji silk, canton gauze and silk gambiered, silk wears, kerchiefs, embroideries and other ready-made silk products, rayon yarns and other artificial fibres, etc.

	Address	*Cable Address*
Head Office:	*Tung An Men Street, Peking*	CHISICORP PEKING
Shanghai Branch:	17, *Chung Shan Road, E.1, Shanghai*	CHISICORP SHANGHAI
Tientsin Branch:	60, *Tai Erh Chwang Road, Hoshi Ward, Tientsin*	CHISICORP TIENSTIN
Kwangtun Branch:	50, *Pearl River Road, Shameen, Canton*	CHISICANT CANTON
Shantung Branch:	78, *Chung Shan Road, Tsingtao*	CHSILKCORP TSINGTAO

China National Import and Export Corporation

Principal Exports and Imports: Chemicals, pharmaceuticals, medical instruments, fertilizers, dyestuffs and pigments, paints, rubber and rubber products, petroleum and petroleum products.

	Address	*Cable Address*
Head Office:	*Erh Li Kou, Hsi Chiao, Peking*	CNIEC PEKING
Shanghai Branch:	27, *Chung Shan Road, E.1., Shanghai*	CHIMEXCORP SHANGHAI
Tientsin Branch:	171, *Chien Shieh Road, Tientsin*	NOCIMOR TIENTSIN
Canton Branch:	2, *West Bund, Canton*	CHIMPORTCO CANTON
Tsingtao Branch:	82, *Chung Shan Road, Tsingtao*	CNIECTB TSINGTAO

China National Instruments Import Corporation

Principal Exports and Imports: Various scientific instruments, laboratory equipment, electrical and electronic instruments, wired equipment and supplies, wireless equipment and supplies, cinematographical and photographical equipment and supplies, cultural and educational instruments, etc.

	Address	*Cable Address*
Head Office:	*Erh Li Kou, Hsi Chiao, Peking*	INSTRIMPORT PEKING
Shanghai Branch:	27, *Chung Shan Road, E.1., Shanghai*	INSTRIMP SHANGHAI
Tientsin Branch:	14, *Chang Teh Road, Tientsin*	INSTRIMP TIENTSIN
Canton Branch:	2, *West Bund, Canton*	INSTRIMP CANTON

China National Machinery Import Corporation

Principal Exports and Imports: Machine tools, power machinery, mining and metallurgical machinery, electric machinery and equipment, air compressors, hoists and cranes, excavators, precision measuring tools, cutting tools and other tools, etc.

	Address	*Cable Address*
Head Office:	*Erh Li Kou, Hsi Chiao, Peking*	MACHIMPORT PEKING
Shanghai Branch:	27, *Chung Shan Road, E.1., Shanghai*	MACHIMPORT SHANGHAI
Tientsin Branch:	14, *Chang Teh Road, Tientsin*	MACHIMPORT TIENTSIN
Canton Branch:	2, *West Bund, Canton*	MACHINERY CANTON
Tsingtao Branch:	82, *Chung Shan Road, Tsingtao*	MACHIMPORT TSINGTAO

China National Technical Import Corporation

Exports and Imports: Whole-plant projects and equipment.

Address	*Cable Address*
Erh Li Kou, Hsi Chiao, Peking	TECHIMPORT PEKING

China National Transport Machinery Import Corporation

Principal Exports and Imports: Transport and agricultural machinery (various motor vehicles and parts thereof; locomotives, ships, agricultural machinery and parts thereof), printing machines, machinery for pharmaceutical, food, architectural, chemical and other light industries.

	Address	Cable Address
Head Office:	Erh Li Kou, Hsi Chiao, Peking	TRANSMACH PEKING
Shanghai Branch:	27, Chung Shan Road, E.1., Shanghai	TRANSMACH SHANGHAI
Tientsin Branch:	14, Chang Teh Road, Tientsin	TRANSMACH TIENTSIN
Canton Branch:	2, West Bund, Canton	TRANSMACH CANTON
Tsingtao Branch:	82, Chung Shan Road, Tsingtao	TRANSMACH TSINGTAO

China National Metals Import Corporation

Principal Exports and Imports: Ferrous alloys, profiled steels, steel tubes, cast iron pipes, steel plates and sheets, railway materials, non-ferrous raw materials and rolled materials, metallic semi-finished products, iron wire, wire-nails, etc.

	Address	Cable Address
Head Office:	Erh Li Kou, Hsi Chiao, Peking	CHIMETALS PEKING
Shanghai Branch:	27, Chung Shan Road, E.1., Shanghai	CHIMETALS SHANGHAI
Tientsin Branch:	171, Chien Shieh Road, Tientsin	CHIMETALS TIENTSIN
Canton Branch:	2, West Bund, Canton	CHIMETALS CANTON
Tsingtao Branch:	82,Chung Shan Road, Tsingtao	CHIMETALS TSINGTAO

China National Foreign Trade Transportation Corporation

Main Business handled: (1) Arranging customs clearance and deliveries of cargoes imported, exported and/or re-exported by sea, land, air and post. (2) Acting as agents on authorization for arranging shipments of transit cargoes at Chinese ports and forwarding imported cargoes. (3) Arranging marine and transportation insurance and instituting claims on behalf of cargo owners.

	Address	Cable Address
Head Office:	Erh Li Kou, Hsi Chiao, Peking	SINOTRANS PEKING
Shanghai Branch:	74, Tienchih Road, Shanghai	SINOTRANS SHANGHAI
Tientsin Branch:	172, Liaoning Road, Tientsin	SINOTRANS TIENTSIN
Tangku Sub-Branch:	44, Hsinkang Road, Tangku, Hopei	SINOTRANS TANGKU
Chinwangtao Sub-Branch:	Kailin Road, Chinwangtao, Hopei	6866 CHINWANGTAO
Canton Branch:	2, West Bund, Canton	5931 CANTON
Whampoa Sub-Branch:	Whampoa Port, Canton	SINOTRANS WHAMPOA
Tsamkong Sub-Branch:	Tsamkong Port, Kwangtung	8319 TSAMKONG
Tsingtao Branch:	82, Chung San Road, Tsingtao	6586 TSINGTAO
Dairen Branch:	16, Stalin Road, Dairen	7120 DAIREN

Sinofracht Ship Chartering and Broking Corporation

Main Business handled: Arranging the chartering of vessels and booking of shipping space required for the carriage of State's import and export cargoes; Chartering vessels and booking shipping space for principals home and abroad as per authorization; Canvassing cargoes for shipowners.

Address	*Cable Address*
Erh Li Kou, Hsi Chiao, Peking	SINOFRACHT PEKING

China Resources Company

Hongkong Agency for the China National Corporations as listed above.

Address	*Cable Address*
Bank of China Building, Hongkong	CIRECO HONGKONG

CHINESE MINISTRIES CONCERNED WITH FINANCE, TRADE AND PRODUCTION

Ministry of Finance,
    10, Kung An Chieh, Inside Ch'ienmen, Peking.
First Ministry of Commerce,
    82, Chuan Te Hutung, Hsi Ssu Pai Lou, Peking.
Second Ministry of Commerce,
        (*formerly Ministry of City Services*)
    Sau Li Ho, Outside Fu Hsing Men, Peking.
Ministry of Foreign Trade,
    Tung Ch'ang An Chieh, Peking.
Ministry of Food,
    44, Shih Fuma Ta Chieh, Hsi Tan District, Peking.
Ministry of Geology,
    Yang Shih Ta Chieh, Hsi Ssu Pai Lou, Peking.
Ministry of the Metallurgical Industry,
    26, Tung Chiao Min Hsiang, Tung Tan District, Peking.
First Ministry of Machine Building,
        (*incorporating former Second Ministry of Machine Building and Ministry of the Electrical Equipment Industry*),
    54, Pei Ho Yen, Tung Tan District, Peking.
Second Ministry of Machine Building,
        (*formerly Third Ministry of Machine Building*),
    Building No. 4, Hsi Yuan Hotel, Erh Li Hou, West Suburb, Peking.
Ministry of Water Conservancy and Electric Power,
        (*formerly separate Ministries*),
    Hoping Men Nei, Peking.
Ministry of the Petroleum Industry,
    Liu Pu Keng, Outside Kuang An Men, Peking.
Ministry of the Coal Industry,
    Tung Chang in Chieh, Peking.

Ministry of the Chemical Industry,
  1, Hoping Y Lu, Outside Antingmen, Peking.
Ministry of Light Industry,
        (*now incorporates Ministry of the Food Industry*),
  Chan Lan Kuan Lu, Outside Fu Ch'eng Men, Peking.
Ministry of Aquatic Products,
  Building No. 2, Hsi Yuan Hotel, Erh, Li Kou West Suburb, Peking.
Ministry of Building,
        (*now incorporates the Ministry of Building Materials, the Ministry
        of City Construction, and part of the abolished National Construction
        Commission*),
  Pai Wan Chuang, West Suburb, Peking.
Ministry of Railways,
  Tung Ch'ang An Chieh, Peking.
Ministry of Communications,
  1, Pei Ping Ma Ssu, Chiao Tao Kou Nan Ta Chieh, Peking.
Ministry of Posts and Telecommunications,
  Hsi Ch'ang An Chieh, Peking.
Ministry of Agriculture,
  1, Lao Ch'ien Chu, Tung Tan District, Peking.
Ministry of State Farms and Land Reclamation,
  1, Lao Ch'ien Chu, Tung Tan District, Peking.
Ministry of Forestry,
        (*now incorporates Ministry of Timber Industry*),
  Hoping Li, Outside Anting Men, Peking.
Ministry of Public Health,
  Hou Hai, Ku Lou, Peking.
Ministry of the Textile Industry,
  Tung Ch'and An Chieh, Peking.
State Planning Commission,
        (*now incorporates part of the abolished National Construction
        Commission*),
  Sau Li Ho, West Suburb, Peking.
State Technological Commission,
  Sau Li Ho, West Suburb, Peking.
National Economic Commission,
        (*now includes part of the abolished National Construction
        Commission*),
  Pai Wan Chuang, West Suburb, Peking.

Index

Note: references to specific commodities, countries, areas, etc., in the list of Sovnarkhozy (Book I, Part II) and the statistical tables have not been indexed.

Advertising, 22, 114, 166, 172
Agents, forwarding, 166, 167, 168, 170, 178, 179
Agricultural 'circles', 136
Agricultural machinery, 26, 50, 152, 165, 168, 170, 177
Aid, see Underdeveloped countries
Aircraft, 169, 172
Albania, 144
Allocation of materials, 16, 20
Alloys, 165, 168, 171, 178
Aluminium, 40, 41, 42, 50
Anglo-Russian trade agreement, 1959, 124-127;
    list of possible purchases, 128-130
Animal products, 166, 167, 172, 175
Animals, live, see Livestock
Apparatus, scientific and laboratory, 165, 169, 172, 177
Arbitration, 113
Arcos, 117
Art, works of, 166, 167, 173
Australia, 42
Autarky, 20, 21, 40

Bacon, 41, 42
Barter, 34, 167, 169
Bilateralism, 25-27, 33
Board of Trade, see Trade, Board of
Books, 166, 167, 171
Boycott (US of China), 52
British Industry and Engineering (Russian language journal), 22, 115
Building materials and equipment, 165, 166, 168, 171, 172, 173, 177
Bulgaria, 47, 144, 172-173

Cables, 165, 168, 173
Canada, 22, 24
Capital goods, Export prospects of, 46, 47-48
Centralisation, 17, 22, 107
Ceramics, 168, 170
Chemicals, 44, 49, 123, 152, 165, 166, 167, 170, 171, 172, 177
Chiang Kai-shek, 147-148

China, 15, 22, 23, 26, 35, 40, 41, 47, 51-53, 107, 110, 112, 114, 147-152, 161-162, 173-180
China's "great leap forward", 52
Chinese communes, 149
Chinese exports, 41, 51-52
Cinema, equipment, 165, 177;
    films, 166, 168, 171
Clothing, 23, 36, 49, 167
Coal, 17, 26, 49, 123-124, 134, 169, 173, 176
Cocoa, 21, 175
Cocom, 113
Co-efficients, system of, 156
Coffee, 175
Collective farms, 17, 24, 124, 135, 138, 141
Comecon, 25-26, 108, 132
Comparative advantage, 22, 23, 31
Competitive co-existence, 57, 160
Computors, 49
Consumer choice, 18, 19
Consumer goods, 19, 36, 49-50, 111
Contract terms, 113
Convertibility of rouble, see Rouble convertibility
Copper, 21
Costs (see also Comparative costs) 17, 18, 23
Cotton, 22, 51, 166, 172, 173
Credits, problem of, 44, 113
Czechoslovakia, 15, 26, 31, 35, 39, 40, 47, 49, 101-104, 110, 136-138, 169-170

Diamonds, 37, 50
Dillon, 56
Discrimination, 26, 42
Dumping, 24, 25, 35, 36

Eccles Mission, see Anglo-Soviet trade agreement
Economic regions, see Regional Economic Councils
Electrical appliances, 169, 171, 173
Electricity, 18, 110
Enterprise, productive, 14, 16
Excavators, 50, 177

181

Exchange rates, 23, 32
Export Credits Guarantee Department, 113, 157
Export prices, see Prices
Export surpluses of communist countries, 36, 40, 50-51
External prices, see Prices

Factories, complete, 167, 170, 173
Fertilisers, see Chemicals
Films, see Cinema
Fish, 35, 167, 172, 175
Flax, 51, 166
Footwear, 22, 35, 39, 53, 171
Ford Motor Company, 112
France, 36
Free trade, 116
Fruit, 168, 172, 175
Furniture, 19, 49, 171, 172
Furs, 39, 166, 169, 172, 174

Gas, natural, 17, 123
Germany, East, 26, 33, 47, 49, 94-97, 109, 142-144
Germany, West, 42, 142, 143-144
Gold, 41, 44-45
Gosplan, 14, 15, 21, 115
Grain, 24, 51, 166, 171, 172
Great Britain, 21, 23, 33, 35, 112

Hungarian uprising, 139
Hungary, 20, 31, 110, 139-142

Iceland, 35
Import priorities, China's, 52, 152
Imports, requirements of Soviet countries, 21, 48-50
India, 25, 35
Input-output analysis, 17
Integration, 108, 110
Intourist, see Travel
Investment plans, 23
Iron, 26, 33, 50, 124, 178
Italy, 42

Japan, 52, 53
Jugoslav export/import organisations, directory of, 155
Jugoslav price system, 32
Jugoslavia, 32, 107, 144, 153-157
Jute, 21

Khrushchev, 119, 120, 132, 160

Leather, 166, 169, 170, 171, 172, 174
Licences, import and export, 121, 122, 155-156
Livestock, 166, 167, 171, 172, 174, 175

Machine tools, 50, 161, 165, 168, 171, 177
Mao Tse-tung, 148
Marshall Plan, 26, 108, 131, 132
Massey-Ferguson, 156
Mining equipment, 26, 165, 166, 167, 177
Ministries, Chinese, 150, 179-180
Ministry of Foreign Trade, 21, 34, 115, 116, 121, 150
Moscow Economic Conference, 118
"Most Favoured Nation" treatment, 34-37
Motor vehicles, 26, 51, 156, 165, 168, 171, 172, 177
Multilateralism, 33, 34
Music, 166, 167, 173

National income, 30
Norway, 35

Oil, 18, 26, 33, 41, 42, 43, 50, 123-124, 144, 166, 168, 171, 172, 177
Oil pipelines, network of, 26, 50, 110, 133
Oil production, 50
Oilseeds, 53, 166, 175
Over-centralised state, 119

Paintings, see Art
Paper, 26, 165, 168, 171, 173
Patents, Communist attitude to, 43, 114
Petrol, see Oil
Pig-iron, 40, 51, 123, 171, 176
Plan fulfilment, 16, 19, 20
Planning of foreign trade, 21-22
Plastics, 168, 171
Poland, 23, 26, 30, 39, 40, 49, 98-100, 109, 133-136, 167-169
Price fixing, domestic, 17, 23-24, 29-30
Price fixing, export, 23, 30-31, 109
Price reform, 24
Prices, export, 23-24, 30-31, 109; external, 23; retail, 18; wholesale, 18; world, 23
Printing, 165, 169, 172, 178
Priorities of production, 109
Profit margins, 17

Quantitative planning, 21

Railway rolling stock and equipment, 23, 26, 39, 152, 165, 166, 168, 171, 178
Reciprocity, 35, 36
Reforms, economic, 1957, 15
Regional economic councils, 15, 22, 61-86

Retail prices, see Prices
Rice, 23, 53, 175
Rouble convertibility, 45; revaluation, effect of, 109
Roumania, 26, 36, 110, 144, 171-172
Rubber, 21, 43, 165, 169, 171, 172

Self-sufficiency (see also Autarky), 48, 108
Ships and shipbuilding, 21, 165, 167, 170, 171, 177
Sino-Soviet trade agreement, 110, 149; 1950 Treaty, 148
Sovnarkhozy, see Regional economic councils
Sports goods, 169, 173
Stalin, influence of, 56, 119
Stamps, 166, 167
State trading corporations (for commodities handled see individual product references), 13, 24-26, 165-179
Steel, 16, 18, 19, 50, 110, 123, 152, 165, 167, 168, 171, 173, 178
Strategic embargoes, 43, 112
Sugar, 33, 168, 169, 172
Switzerland, 112, 150

Tariff duties, 35
Tax direct, 18; turnover, 18, 19
Tea, 175
Telecommunications, 152, 165, 168
Television, 169

Textiles, 19, 23, 53, 167, 168, 169, 170, 171, 172, 176
Timber, 14, 16, 21, 40, 51, 124, 165, 168, 170, 171, 173
Tin, 25, 42, 176
Tito, 153-154
Tobacco, 166, 171, 172, 173
Tractors, 50, 152, 156, 165
Trade, Board of, 36, 112-113; commercial relations and exports dept., 122; export services branch, 157; journal, 113
Trade corporations, see State trading corporations
Trade delegations, 14, 121
Trade fairs, 145
Trade statistics, 90-104
Trade, technique of 24-26, 115
Travel, 123, 151, 167
Trusts, Czechoslovakian, 16

Underdeveloped countries, trade with, 26, 47-48
USA, 33, 43, 55-56, 112, 123

Watches, 51, 169
Wheat, 22, 23-24, 25, 33, 40, 49, 175
Wholesale prices, see Prices
Wireless, 51, 168, 169, 177
Wool, 21, 43, 166, 172, 173, 174
World prices, see Prices

Yugoslavia, see Jugoslavia

For Product Safety Concerns and Information please contact our
EU representative GPSR@taylorandfrancis.com Taylor & Francis
Verlag GmbH, Kaufingerstraße 24, 80331 München, Germany